UNHEARD TESTIMONY

Unheard Testimony

McKnight VS. General Motors

M.C. Knight

To order additional copies of this book, contact:
Xlibris Corporation
1-888-795-4274
www.Xlibris.com
Orders@Xlibris.com
32464

Contents

PREFACE

"When power leads a man toward arrogance, poetry reminds him of his limitations. When Power narrows the areas of man's concern, poetry reminds him of the richness and diversity of existence. When power corrupts, poetry cleanses, for art establishes the basic human truths which must serve as the touchstone of our Judgment."

—John Fitzgerald Kennedy

FOREWORD

Primarily, it is the United States Congress and the Executive Branch that have the power to enact laws as expressed in Articles I and VII of the United States Constitution. For any Bill to become law in the United States of America, it must pass both Houses of Congress and be signed by the President of the United States, or secured by a passing of two-thirds majority of both Houses to override a presidential veto. The Executive Branch and Congress are bound by the language of the statute once created, as stated by the U.S. Supreme Court in INS v. Chadha, 462 U.S. 919, 947 (1983). Quite simply, law making is a power to be shared by both Houses and the President of the United States.

The power of law making by the U.S. Congress and the President of the United States is one aspect of the essence of what the law means and how it should be applied. It is the responsibility of the U.S. courts to reasonably interpret and carry out the law within the proximity of its meaning.

The Office of the President of the United States is an extremely important position and harnesses tremendous authority. On November 3, 1992, one time Arkansas Governor, Bill Clinton, was chosen by the American people as this nation's 42nd President. The newly elected President Bill Clinton would be the first Democrat to gain the White House since 1976, since former President Jimmy Carter. The election of Bill Clinton put an end to the 12-year Republican authority in the White House.

In April of 1992, George Bush, then President of the United States, was summoned by the three U.S. automotive leaders, General Motors, Ford and Chrysler, who once dominated the automotive industry worldwide, to strike an accord with Japan to provide a more equitable trade environment for the industry as a whole and to provide the same reciprocity for trade to the U.S. automotive industry.

During these intense trade negotiations, President George Bush would suddenly collapsed without warning and shortly thereafter recovered. This was quickly categorized as a brief medical occurrence. Initially, this appeared to be a serious and mysterious affliction or phenomenon. The occurrence sparked concerns about the President's condition.

At the conclusion of the trade accord, the three U.S. automotive companies expressed dissatisfaction with the agreement reached between President Bush, as the key spokesperson for the U.S. automotive group, and Japan. President Bush had indicated this was the beginning of further progress to be made in trade agreements with Japan and other countries. This responsibility would be one of many to be relinquished to the newly elected President Bill Clinton.

Ross Perot, the self-financed independent and Texas businessman, captured one-sixth of the American electorate during his bid for the Office of the Presidency. Perot financed a very aggressive campaign for this office. Throughout the campaign, several revelations of each candidate surfaced for consideration and scrutiny by the American people. The corporate relationship between General Motors Corporation and Mr. Perot came into question and was addressed during his campaign. The same is true of those Mr. Perot was running against.

As we know, Mr. Perot entered General Motors Corporation in 1984 as a result of GM's decision to purchase Electronic Data Systems (EDS) Corporation from its founder and major shareholder, Ross Perot, for the purpose of helping to solve some of GM's operational problems. Somehow, by December of 1986, the relationship had grown sour. General Motors had decided to part ways with Mr. Perot, as decided by General Motors' then chairman Roger Smith. Although Mr. Perot was at odds with General Motors Corporation, on the surface his battle with the giant automotive company was short-lived as a result of an arrangement between General Motors Corporation and Mr. Perot, without any significant litigation.

Other significant controversial issues also surfaced during the campaign. One most notably was that of our legal system today, given its conservative posture during the Bush administration and the implications and effects of its findings and determinations.

General Motors Corporation has had other notable contenders such as Delorean, Nader and perhaps Iaccoca, however, such challenges were outside a U.S. courtroom.

This material will provide for the first time an account of the trials and tribulations of contending with the world's most powerful corporation by an individual, McKnight, within and outside the proscriptions of law—a conquest which could happen to any man, woman or child of these United States of America. This involvement provides further enhancement and insights for those who desire and practice law.

INTRODUCTION

Milwaukee is a town predominated by German and Polish descendants with strong cultural ties to their mother countries; a town besieged with political and social difficulty as aired by CBS Network's "Sixty Minutes" and also reflected in the town's daily newspapers about dissensions that exist between various treaty protestors regarding the rights of the Indian tribes in the North. Here you will find one of General Motors Corporation's youngest executives standing up against the world's most influential company in an environment where the company itself has an established presence quite different from what the executive was accustomed to.

This young executive was educated and grew up in the surrounding New York metropolitan area. He attended school in New York and New Jersey and completed his Master's degree in Wisconsin after being relocated to a General Motors Division. A very young corporate executive, he was enriched with business savvy and natural ability, and perhaps envied by other managers for his finesse and potential to ascend to the highest possible level in the company. A very hard working and enterprising young man, he had to eventually forsake ten years—his best years—to contend with the world's most powerful organization in and out of court.

One of the youngest executive managers to engage in strife with the giant automotive General Motors Corporation, McKnight showed GM firsthand his ability to endure what seemed to be an everlasting bout of challenge, negotiation and leadership. He directed the development and coordination of credible information and provided administration to those who represented him before the courts. He focused on various alternatives to champion his involvement with the huge company—litigation which would ultimately reach the fourteenth floor office of Chairman Roger Smith's at General Motors in Detroit, and beyond.

What are some of the things you can expect as an individual suddenly confronted with having to litigate against a massive organization or company. This material will provide insight as to what you can expect in matters of this kind.

The General Motors Corporation was determined to completely destroy this talented young executive within and outside its organization as evidenced by the malicious and outrageous assertions made by their legal counsel during courtroom trials. The young executive found himself in a legal arena filled with uncertainty because of the changing United States Supreme Court judges, mostly appointed during Ronald Reagan and George Bush's Presidencies. The court suddenly appeared more conservative as it attempted to clarify laws established in the year 1866 for the protection of workers and their relationships with their employers regarding employee entitlements for infractions caused by the employers. The court determined what was available to any individual who may have to rely on the statutes as a case is structured by his attorney. The United States Congress realized there were substantial limitations to a person's entitlements from their employer under these statutes, and drafted a 1990 Bill which ultimately was vetoed by President George Bush. President Bush then submitted his own Bill which was later rejected by Congress. Congress wanted to establish new laws that would provide substance to the old ones in order to discourage deliberate wrongdoing by a company.

This young executive was up against the awesome legal fortitude of the General Motors Corporation, its known and unknown legal affiliates. He would be caught in the revolving door of legal and administrative reforms with rather substantial limitations. He had grown accustomed to street fights in his earlier days in New York, but they did not compare to the various abuses he suffered while at the General Motors Corporation—even though he had consistently operated in the best interest of the company and had provided substantial contributions to the organization. The battle continues in a backyard familiar to the enormous General Motors organization.

CHAPTER I

The Assignment

The information contained in this writing is a true account of the facts and circumstances as they occurred during one of General Motors' youngest manager's challenge with the company. This challenge lasted more than a decade before administrative, State and Federal tribunals, as well as before the Seventh Circuit Appeals Court and the United State Supreme Court, and back again. This process provided additional encumbrances because of the way the legislation was fashioned. This book contains factual chronicles of occupational incidents, industrial murder and a potential industrial accident. However, without discouragement, and as not to be intimidated, I continued my quest to accomplish my objectives for the benefit of all individuals who at some point in their lives may be confronted with such a challenge—testing the operants of the law at all cost, in order to correct a wrong under this country's legal system. The attorneys assigned to represent General Motors Corporation were from the largest law firm of its kind in the state. They harnessed more than 150 lawyers who developed a very aggressive defense enriched with negative implications to completely devastate me, as if I were a Ross Perot, Ralph Nader, John Delorean or Lee Iaccoca.

Every opportunity for settlement was provided for the giant General Motors Corporation, but they refused to relinquish and quickly settle all matters scheduled for litigation. General Motors Corporation is the world's largest and most powerful company. They knew this environment well. They did not have to settle this case as they knew their way through this legal maze at the direction of their enormous staff of lawyers. This gave them the a legal competitive advantage over me, since I had never been in this environment before.

This involvement could be viewed as a form of corporate punishment for me since General Motors and its attorneys were relentless in their attempts to successfully defend GM and to claim victory. However, General Motors representatives often say they only hire the best. They know this before the person is hired because they conduct background investigations. This massive organization realized it was not up against one of their ordinary executive managers but one of its most talented.

Before I completed my legal involvement with GM, some of the country's most notorious trials would also be completed, such as those of Michael Milken, Ivan Boesky, Mike Tyson, Claus Von Bulow, the Iran-Contra affair and the Senate's confirmation hearing of Supreme Court Judge Clarence Thomas.

I was faced with a pretext of deception conducted by several individuals out to destroy my career, reputation and presence with the giant automotive company. Perhaps they were laying the groundwork to conduct future assaults against others so similarly situated. The company utilized as much might as it possessed to undermine my foundation of alternatives and attempted to completely devastate me in the face of the courts. I was to undertake this challenge without having resources equal to those of General Motors.

This kind of confrontation and litigation would devastate the feeble minded and distress those whose condition grew ancient. In essence, this was a form of intellectual martial arts. This involvement has profound psychological implications associated with the challenges against such a massive organization. Although I suddenly found myself in just another street fight, I stood my ground. What happened here could happen to anyone who decides to challenge his company, however, I must say General Motors is exceptional because of its finesse, size and influence. Quite simply, General Motors is by far no ordinary company.

The authority of the huge automotive company reached well beyond the corporate walls of General Motors. Eventually the implications and effects of this legal battle touched my family and friends, both directly and indirectly.

In order to lessen the financial damages caused by the colossal General Motors Corporation, I was able to find work in the Wall Street environment and become a successful executive there. This environment has fostered the likes of Carl Ichan, Marvin Davis, and Irwin Jacobs, as well as Sir Robert Maxwell, Michael Milken, Warren Buffet and Ivan Boesky. As I continued my contention with General Motors regarding the interference with my career advancement and position with the company, I was able to develop significant relationships and substantial large investment transactions of hundreds of millions of dollars through hard work.

Throughout my involvement, I did not discuss the case or tell anyone that I was involved in contention with General Motors. I did not disclose any of GM's most confidential trade secrets. However, General Motors attempted to make certain of that in many regards—for one, they sought to undermine my credibility and cast a shadow of doubt on my loyalty to the company. Someone did not want me to continue my professional development and successful accomplishments. Mysteriously, I experienced an unexpected, nonrecurring episode of fatigue which built up during one of my tenures in the financial area of General Motors where I was assigned.

It appeared as if the giant General Motors Corporation was holding me against a wall of legal controversy, delivering the blows of the system as others watched. Others attempted to establish an allegiance with the wealthy organization, a relationship I once held and which was deliberately placed in jeopardy by those who did not want to see me succeed there, or for that matter, anywhere. Somehow, extremely important evidence concerning my performance, which my attorney had in his possession more than a couple years, was not allowed to go before a jury. Several key witnesses were not put on the stand to give their testimonies.

At times it seemed as if this entire involvement had been deliberately orchestrated from the very beginning to forestall my rise to the top of the giant automotive company and eventually destroy me. I was subjected to severe conditions of adversity to crush my enthusiasm and motivation. Often, I was provoked by others. Not only was I one of GM's best managers, as attested to under oath by witnesses, but I was also one of their most qualified executives and could have been one of the youngest corporate leaders to take charge of it as president.

It seemed as if the very system set up to discourage companies from engaging in adverse practices or cause deliberate harm to anyone was causing me additional injury. General Motors and their attorneys knew it would be difficult for me because of the scheduling of the trials, technicalities in the law, and the lengthy delays, to receive what I was awarded before the courts and to take the case to higher levels. Here, attorneys, without my presence, began to lose back portions of the judgment I secured. In essence, I had to grapple with and encourage my attorney to go forward to trial with my case.

I began to feel resentment against me for pursuing my constitutional rights. The powerful General Motors Corporation appeared to have devastated the attorney who represented a fellow co-worker in a different trial of a similar matter. This seemed to completely undermine his confidence in himself and cause him to lose sight of the realities of this case. Before this, the attorney had lost his Circuit Court trial as well as his District Court trial for the other General Motors employee he had represented. And now this same attorney was to represent me and begin my trial.

At a meeting my attorney scheduled a couple days before my scheduled trial, he highly recommended I consider a rather insignificant offer. At that moment, as you can imagine, I completely lost my composure and had to remember he was not the adversary. I did not wish to think so, for the sake of things. I did not want to believe my own attorney would deceive me at this time. Hell, no . . . he could not have.

I knew then that I had to take charge of my case and provide the attorney with the direction he needed to win. He would fight me every step of the way. However, I realized I needed someone with a law degree—someone I could direct. Give me anyone with a law degree who is simply not afraid of challenge. The attorney shouted uncontrollably as I left his office, "You're going to lose, McKnight! You're going to lose! McKnight, McKnight, you're going to lose!"

I realized he was reacting to his previous losses and the power and influence of GM's lawyers. I told him he would continue the litigation as scheduled. In addition, I responded to his earlier reply that I was going to lose that he was forgetting one important fact of evidence: Me!

"You are simply wrong," I said. I had continued to have confidence in him as an attorney who needed some direction. It seemed as if he resented me for providing him with direction and insisting he litigate accordingly. Generally, it is not commonplace for me to be forceful to the extent of losing my composure and dignity. Besides, most responsible people who work with and for me usually accomplish my objectives. There was absolutely no turning back. After all, I was deeply involved in a most difficult challenge with a highly influential company, an overwhelming task for most people. I gathered I was not out of line in regard to my extremely firm stance with my attorney, as General Motors did have some time to polish me as a responsive manager. However, some of the rough edges were beginning to show through.

The entire process appeared as if it were designed to hinder my rise to the very top of the General Motors Company at an early age. The mentality of the people involved was such that they probably would have destroyed the careers of a Michael Jackson, Bruce Springsteen, Michael Jordan, Madonna, or Ross Perot, although these individuals are from a different cast altogether. The people who were behind their success need to be highly commended as they encouraged and fostered their development to the ultimate form of success. These people are to be commended for their interest in developing these people to whom and what they are today. (There exists a host of other talented people in their chosen fields and own right who have been developed by others that I did not include here for many reasons.)

Tangible information was initially presented before the courts to establish and confirm the existence of a conspiracy against me. The system continued to victimize me, causing substantial delays in paying me my judgment and in considering other legal entitlements. This treatment began to cause additional substantial discomfort to me and my family. Adding to our discomfort was concern over the act of murder carried out by one of the sons of the last manager for whom I had worked. However, I had no choice but to wait it out, go toe to toe with General Motors and continue fighting the issues of a cause I did not initiate.

Although I knew I had a corporate price on my head, I was not able to determine where or from whom my release would come. It was the calm before the storm.

Then, one day in July in a credit office of General Motors located in a southeastern community, a customer went on a rampage. After having several discussions with General Motors customer service representatives regarding the status of his account and the need for them to repossess his vehicle, he apparently was very angered. He began shooting at will at the facility and killed several individuals including himself. Their actions must have angered him and he demonstrated his frustrations about how he had been treated during the process of repossessing his vehicle.

Similar mass shootings outside the General Motors organization were repeated throughout this decade of litigation by those who were not able to contain their frustrations to a courtroom where justice should be provided.

On another occasion, within General Motors Corporation, two janitors took it upon themselves to conduct a private execution of one of their co-workers. Mysterious circumstances also surrounded an unexplained injury which I myself experienced during assignment inside the walls of General Motors. On many occasions I felt nauseous and light-headed at work several hours after arriving in the financial area of the company, where I was not completely accepted by my immediate peer group as I had been by the rest of the organization before assignment there. This was perhaps due to envy of my qualifications by the others in the financial work group where I was assigned.

The manager at General Motors Corporation, who would ultimately play a key role in the elimination of my position without proper authorization, was victimized by his son's involvement in the conspiratory murder of his boss, who had a position similar to mine. His son carried out the deliberate and premeditated murder during a third shift operation at the plant where he worked. I was also asked to work a third shift operation at General Motors Corporation. His father, my immediate superior, was the same person who turned his head when the defendant's brother came close to hitting me with his vehicle during an early morning work assignment. He also did not support my disciplinary action of verbal and written reinstruction to operate this vehicle more safely in a heavy pedestrian area in the plant.

My immediate superior, Eric, worked for and reported to Denis Cronk, who was a named defendant in the McKnight v. General Motors case. My attorney, however, seemed to present the accident issue only casually and would not show outrageous conduct regarding the incident before the jury. I was more fortunate to see what was coming regarding my potential industrial accident. The young man who lost his life on that evening, murdered by my boss's son, was not as fortunate to survive his injuries and fate. The local newspaper reported this murder, stating that the body was found in a 55-gallon container by a sanitation worker who hauled away industrial waste. The worker noticed a human hand dropping out of the drum as he began to load discarded materials into his truck. I remembered my boss had walked among the 55-gallon containers in my work area on the morning of my incident at work. His son perhaps concluded a jury would never believe a dead man. The jury in my case initially did not fully establish liability as measured by damages, because of legal technicalities, though I told nothing but the truth to the jury.

It was in General Motors' interest to keep Eric on following the disclosure of his son's direct involvement in the murder and plan to profit from the victim's life insurance policy, as revealed in the local newspaper. General Motors, I was told by my co-workers, promoted and transferred Eric to Australia to wait for the appearance of subsequent trials of McKnight v. General Motors. Following Eric's son's involvement in the murder of his immediate superior, I did not understand the company's position; I had done nothing to justify the elimination of my position with the company without authorization, according to corporate procedure. This was purely an act of naked aggression on his part. Perhaps he would have liked to end my involvement in the General Motors case by stuffing me in a 55-gallon container as his son did. (In fact, he would have had one hell of a time doing it.) Perchance a forensic psychologist could explain the connection.

Chapter II

Rude Awakenings

In June of 1978, I was recruited from the New York-New Jersey metropolitan area by General Motors. Prior to General Motors' recruitment, I had just completed the purchase of real estate approximately five miles from the Liberty Park area, across from New York Harbor, surrounded by Ellis Island and the Statue of Liberty, and had negotiated with my realtor and attorneys for the purchase of a couple more dwellings. In addition, I had almost completed my Master's degree in Taxation, at the age of 25, making me the first in my family to receive a college degree, let alone a Master's. Although I was doing administrative work as well as working in the area of taxation and doing audit work for a New York certified public accounting firm, I decided to make an investment in an entertainment facility. It was my objective to completely renovate the facility and turn it into an elegant restaurant, recording studio and entertainment center. My partner, Mike O'Gorman, and myself had developed a master plan to rapidly expand our operations.

This all came to a standstill when I decided to accept employment with General Motors Corporation. It had been my desire to work for General Motors since a very early age, and finally the opportunity was before me. My meeting with General Motors Corporation was conducted at the Americana Hotel in New York City. Larry and Renee, two executives from General Motors, had chosen me for the corporate position in their management ranks. I had also received offers from two other well known corporations, Exxon and IBM. It appeared as if this were a relatively simple life assignment—to be chosen to work for a premier company. However, you sometimes do not know, regardless of how talented you are or potentially may become, who does not want you to exist.

I was very impressed with the way Larry and Renee conducted themselves in a well-regarded, professional manner. My discussions with them were in one of New York's finest establishments and in the company of another young female candidate who was considering an assignment with General Motors Corporation. Larry and Renee told us that our assignments would be for two to three years in Wisconsin. Thereafter we could consider other assignment locations and were not limited to returning to the New York metropolitan area if we did not wish to after the time in Wisconsin.

Everything that evening was just perfect. My confidence level, as well as my enthusiasm, was very high, and conversation was without flaw. My presence was at its best. I knew that the entire day and evening had gone well. The executives had provided me with very enlightening insights into General Motors Corporation. We had held several different conversations throughout the evening, ranging from sports and theater to corporate interests.

At the end of the evening, both executives provided invitations to visit their corporate facility located in Wisconsin. They described this particular facility as the West Point of General Motors. The GM executives indicated they wanted to provide me the opportunity to work for their company. They indicated I would be required to work for the company as a manager for two to three years at the Wisconsin facility and then I would perhaps be in a position to transfer back to the New York area. Perhaps I would work in their financial area in New York or New Jersey. They indicated I would have to work as a manager in their manufacturing organization first in order to learn the business from an operational standpoint and provided several insights about the responsibilities required. I was certain I would not have any problems. I am an exceptionally unyielding person when it comes to work and can be considered a workaholic.

At the time I was made this offer to work for General Motors Corporation, I was being made similar offers from Exxon and IBM, also out-of-state. I accepted the position with General Motors. However, I had engaged in conversation with another executive from a different company regarding his thoughts as to which company I should eventually work for. He said that General Motors Corporation would not be the place for me to work because of my level of professionalism and credentials. He felt I would fit in more with IBM. But, as I said earlier, I always had a desire to work for General Motors from a very young age, and now I had the opportunity to work for the largest company on earth. I thought I could work at this location for three years, subsequently transfer back to New York. I could then continue my program of real estate expansion and entertainment development with my business associate, Mike O'Gorman, a former college classmate, friend, and co-worker.

Exxon Corporation flew me to their Houston, Texas location and offered me a position with their organization in their financial area. However, this would have been a permanent assignment. I would not be able to return to New York, the city I roamed as a kid and felt was one of the greatest cities in the world.

My decision of attempting to build into an agreement with the company I chose to work for certainly had to do with the level of compensation I was to receive. Quite naturally, the more money offered, the longer I'd be willing to stay. This would also require other corporate perks. Besides, it was not only the compensation that had to be considered, it was the personality of the firm as well. This was very important to me.

My reservations and itinerary were efficiently provided. I flew to Wisconsin three weeks after my meeting with the executives in New York. As I stepped off the plane at Milwaukee's Mitchell Field Airport on a hot July evening around 5:00 p.m., I was greeted by Norm, a very professional, articulate corporate executive from General Motors, who did not appear to be intimidated by my presence and talents. I was dressed in the finest corporate attire from a select men's fashion boutique of New York.

Norm provided a very warm reception as mandated by his own volition. He carried on an extensive conversation with me pertaining to economics, business, sports and theater. He was an exceptional image of professionalism and finesse. He and his wife Mary took me to a fine restaurant in lower Milwaukee. The evening had gone rather splendidly. Norm and his wife seemed to be good, wholesome people. They complemented the image already provided by Larry and Renee. I was sold on General Motors. My early childhood dream had come true. This was a very important day for me.

The following day I interviewed with approximately six managers and met a host of other individuals in the company. It had been a very busy day, and I felt as though I was being confirmed for public office. The general nature of inquiry was: why do you want to work for General Motors Corporation and why should we hire you?

I was provided with similar treatment during my travels with Exxon Corporation and IBM. The executive managers of these companies were quite extensive with their questions as well.

As I went through the interview process at the General Motors facility, I ran into two very difficult interviewers who appeared hostile, especially one manager who remained so. I was able to diffuse the other manager's hostility. There was no noticeable reason why these individuals were hostile. It appeared as if they had a general proclivity of personality toward such behavior. Later, one of them played a key role in this very challenge to come against General Motors Corporation. He acted as if I were violating his position even before I was officially hired by the company. When the interview was completed, I was swiftly taken back to the airport by Renee, one of the executives I had met in New York.

Approximately two weeks later I received a phone call from General Motors representatives offering me the management position. If I accepted, I would have to report to work there within two weeks.

At the same time, I received an offer to work for Exxon Corporation to begin work in 30 days, at which time my semester of graduate school would be completed, and I would receive my degree.

General Motors wanted me to report to their facility as soon as possible. They provided arrangements for me and my family to fly to Wisconsin. We stayed at the Hoffman House Midway Motor Lodge for approximately three and a half weeks while General Motors personnel arranged to have my furniture shipped from New York to Wisconsin. I was moving a second time within 60 days, as I had just purchased my home and the ink was not even dry yet on the closing documents. I decided to keep the house as investment property.

Several other newly recruited managers and salaried personnel stayed at the same hotel. At the end of two weeks' stay I was confronted by a person named Gil Amborn from the accounting organization regarding my expenses and the reason for my stay at the hotel. Gil also played a significant part later in the McKnight v. General Motors trial in the Wisconsin Circuit Court.

I indicated to him I was new to the area and that my furniture was being transferred from the New York area. I simply was unable to move until the first or second week of September, 1978. He appeared to be angered I was provided this accommodation. He wanted to know who had approved it and for how long. I indicated that it was arranged through personnel and manufacturing. He still appeared angry and was very difficult with his line of questioning, more so than any of the other executives, including his boss, Sam, who was in charge of the financial organization.

I simply could not understand his bizarre and unusual line of questioning. I thought it unusual for him to be so hostile since the arrangements had been provided by the company. No one else seemed concerned; my stay at the facilities was within reason.

I asked several other managers and salaried personnel staying at the hotel if they were so questioned by Gil or anyone from the company, but they said they were not. For the life of me I could not understand why I was being treated this way. It appeared as if I had been singled out and treated differently.

My wife and daughter were flown back to the New York-New Jersey area to prepare for the moving of our household effects to Wisconsin by way of a moving service contracted by General Motors.

We searched for a place to stay for approximately two weeks with the assistance of Rocky, an executive in the engineering group at GM. We decided we would select a place to live in Greenfield, a suburb of Milwaukee. The area was fully equipped with many different activities for my family. I was to live on the older Tuckaway golf grounds where they held the Greater Milwaukee Open in past years. This is a popular golfing event held annually in Wisconsin featuring the likes of Gary Player, Arnold Palmer, and many other famous golf celebrities and major contenders.

During my stay in the hotel, I received several phone calls from the executive recruiters from IBM. They left several messages regarding my interest to work for them. However, I thought it would not be ethically correct for me to accept a position with IBM since General Motors had expended a lot in terms of my recruitment and placement with them. Besides, my furniture had been scheduled to be transferred from my home, at last. At this time it had not occurred to me that I would eventually have to contend with GM for any reason whatsoever. In fact, it seemed as if everything was going well.

I left the keys to my house with my parents and asked that they look after my home. My father indicated he would look after my other properties. My plans to continue an aggressive acquisition program and other projects were momentarily put on hold until I could eventually return to the New York-New Jersey area after a few years on assignment with General Motors at the Wisconsin facility. There were some late discussions for assignment on a short-term basis in Flint or Detroit, Michigan, the headquarters of General Motors.

I had approximately one week left in the hotel, as did most of the other executives. Some were to stay longer. I was confronted again about my stay in the Hoffman House Midway Motor Lodge by Gil. Again I explained to him that my stay there had been clearly authorized by the powers that be in the company and that I was actually spending considerably less than what I had been allocated. He wanted to know if I could perhaps arrange to room with one of the other executives in my management group. Several of the other pre-managers offered to allow me to stay with them for the final weeks of my scheduled stay at the hotel. They indicated that their expenses had not been questioned by anyone, and they did not understand why I was being questioned by Gil. I felt very uncomfortable during these conversations with him. The audit conference I had with him was held away from the financial area of the company, in a remote office of the plant some distance from the accounting area where Gil's office was located.

I could not at first understand why I had been centered out. I was at the top of my group, from a performance standpoint, and was situated in a rather unusual circumstance as a newly recruited corporate executive with no friends or relatives in the immediate area. Quite simply, I did not have any family support group as I had back East. At this time I did not have any animosity toward anyone at the company, including Gil, although his inquiries made me feel very uncomfortable. Gil was on the same executive level as I was when he questioned me. Absolutely no one in the company informed me he would be conducting such questioning. I often referred him directly to personnel or other managers of the manufacturing group, mainly Clay. My expense reports were submitted weekly as required.

*   *   *

I began receiving extremely favorable performance ratings regarding my activities during my management group assignment and managed to regain my composure and confidence. I immediately dispelled the negative conference meetings with Gil. I did not feel uncomfortable with the other executives of the company. Initially, I was treated quite well by the other managers. I did my best to limit my involvement with Gil. I did not understand what prompted his concern with me and my expenses, though I suspected it was due to jealousy of my credentials.

I went on accepting new challenges and responsibilities with the company as I was hired to do. I had continued my efforts to provide significant results and contributions for the company. I would walk through the facilities observing many deficiencies in our productive operations. I would then recommend changes that would result in major economic benefits for the company. These recommended improvements, special assignments, proved my ability to lead and manage people effectively, making the organization aware of my existence as a fresh, new contender for more challenging positions with the company. General Motors and their top executives witnessed firsthand my potential as a powerful and influential leader. Later I learned someone did not want my career to flourish within the confines of GM. It almost seemed as if someone had recognized my talents and wanted to contain my development, as my image at some point would be enough to thrust me into a position of tremendous power either within or outside General Motors. I had to be stopped somehow. My image had to be blemished.

When I received my assignment in the management ranks of GM, I was given a grand tour by Norm, one of the executives who interviewed me and with whom I was highly impressed. His method of instruction was very clear and effective. Norm provided me with the insights of the manufacturing organization with regard to what was required of each and every manager.

He complimented the requirements of the manufacturing organization with an elaborate description of the intricacies of the industrial engineering organizations of the company. Manufacturing and other department managers indicated they did not completely understand the people from the financial side of General Motors. They often concluded that the financial people did not completely understand the nature of the business from their perspective, either. However, they understood me very well and liked my approach. I was to fill this void of misunderstanding.

General Motors Corporation historically selected its chairmen, president and several vice presidents and directors from the financial group of the company. At this time my level of motivation was tremendously high. I possessed an objective to work as conscientiously as possible. I knew that hard work, as well as the quality of it, would eventually provide me the opportunity to advance within the company.

It seemed as if the executives of the operational departments of the company were separate from the financial executives, as if they were in a different organization altogether. Although the executives from the other departments I was exposed to felt as if the financial people did not clearly understand them, they were still required to provide financial information regarding their operational performances to them. The information would continue to flow regularly and substantially daily.

The management people of the company wanted to fill this void of misunderstanding as it perhaps would bring the company more completely together. I had a strong background in financial matters, earning superior grades in accounting theory and advanced taxation on the graduate level. I was given a management assignment in the manufacturing organization at General Motors. Throughout my assignment there, I was exposed to many different challenges which required resolution by me. I accepted every challenge with great enthusiasm.

As I operated in an environment filled with 1800 ton presses, highly automated production lines, state of the art robotics, computer systems and electronic welding processes, I began to experience the true art of management and realized the most difficulty was in managing people with respect to the contractual agreement between General Motors and the United Auto Workers Union. However, I demonstrated to the corporation my effectiveness as a manager able to provide leadership and direction for those who worked for me directly and indirectly. I received outstanding production and quality results from my workers, maximizing optimum levels of production and efficient performances in a corporate environment.

Effective management is not an easy task to begin with, since several individuals in the company are competing for the same upper management positions. It is commonplace to find yourself at odds with several managers in the company. There were several I respected and with whom I got along. However, this was just another challenge I welcomed because I knew I was operating in the best interest of the company and my subordinates. General Motors knew this as well. Did General Motors, the company, really care about me and my objectives? Later, it became clear that the company was not as equally committed to me as I was to them. I began to command a high level of respect as I demonstrated the management skills necessary to produce the outstanding results required by the company for our customers. This was shown by the high quantity of products I produced, the quality of my products and the morale of the people who worked for me.

My work area was staffed with new hires, and they had to be trained on production requirements. It is a very involved process to make certain your workers are doing exactly what is needed. Mistakes are very costly, simply because you are mass producing the product at an extremely rapid pace. We produced pollution control equipment, catalytic converters, from a location that equipped every car GM made for use in the United States, as well as for some non-affiliated automotive companies who had to have such equipment on their vehicles before they could sell to their customers. Automobile manufacturers were required to have this equipment or they could not sell their vehicles for use in the United States. Not every automobile manufacturer had the technology as did General Motors. This was a tremendously important product. The ingredients of assembly were highly classified and could not be disclosed to outsiders. The corporation was extremely protective of this information.

The manager of the production operation was accountable to upper management with extremely tight production schedules. There was a very narrow margin of tolerance for obstinateness on the part of the worker. I happened to use a style of management which produced exceptional results. Although at times I, as a manager, would have to resort to disciplining a subordinate worker with cause, I was often able to prove to the Union representatives and our labor organizations that any discipline I imposed was reasonable and necessary. In fact, the Union determined it to be appropriate quite often. My philosophy of what I expected from my workers was quite simple.

On one occasion I was confronted by one of my machine setup operators who was approximately 6'6", 270 pounds. He was frustrated because I had given him some additional work. He was outraged when I required him to clear his machines quickly by himself, without taking other productive workers from their assigned tasks. The request I made was on the fringes of the contract agreement with the Union. He angrily and quickly thrust forward in my direction to within less than arm's length. I simply would not be intimidated by this. I had a job to do and that was all that really mattered to me. I will always stand my ground, I determined.

He stated hostilely that he was not going to do what I had instructed. I immediately reinstructed him to do exactly what I said and not to question my authority again. He then attempted to explain to me that his father was a powerful executive with the company who could make my job very difficult.

I assertively said to him, "I want to make something perfectly clear to you and I do not want you to ever forget it. You can tell this to whomever you desire, including your father. This is my area of responsibility and I will run it as I desire. I couldn't care less if your father were the president of the company. You now work for me and I have a job to do. I hope you understand me completely." I was responsible to this company and ultimately my customers, and we all had a part in this whole scheme of things. I had a job to do and damn it, I was going to do it.

He said one word and I immediately told him he would be placed on notice for possible disciplinary action for failure to obey a direct order, and that any further disobedience or comments could result in a formal reprimand. I suggested he could speak to his committee representative if he wished, but that he should remain quiet until his representative arrived. For the life of me, I could not understand the work ethic here. On the East coast, generally, when people had a job to do they did it without questioning authority. Here it seemed different, as if they wanted to do as they wished. However, I would not tolerate it at all.

This individual conversed with his Union representative that evening. He completed the work as instructed without further conversation with me directly then contacted Personnel. Personnel called me regarding the situation and I provided them with my position regarding the worker's responsibility, keeping in mind the best interest of the employee. Personnel did not have any further questions for me, concluding my involvement and directives with this employee were appropriately handled.

Since I came from the East coast and had been working continuously since the age of 10, I was not accustomed to a subordinate telling his superior what he was and was not going to do. I do not tolerate that attitude from anyone working for me directly or indirectly. Most of the people were hard working; however, there were several individuals like the one described above who would influence others to be difficult workers. Therefore, I prepared myself to go to blows, but only if I could not reason with him. My assignment and responsibilities were very important to me, and I did not want anything to interfere with my objectives or operations.

Several managers concluded it was extremely difficult to manage Union workers effectively and that it took an act of Congress to fire a Union worker and make it stand. This made it difficult for some managers to effectively manage their operations. It is less difficult to manage the executives of General Motors than it is to manage the Union workers because their contractual entitlements seem to be recognized by the company more than a worker's legal rights established by state laws or the U.S. Constitution. General Motors could fire any of its managers and make it stand faster than it could a Union worker.

It is not completely true that it is difficult to effectively manage Union workers. I consistently demonstrated my management ability by striving for high standards, meeting production schedules and requiring excellent efficiency and exceptional quality.

There are several arbitration procedures one must go through with a Union employee before his termination, which discourage the company from terminating the employee. However, for an executive manager of General Motors, the process is rather swift and permanent. The executive is caught between a "rock and a hard place." However, the job must be completed and I made certain of this. Several managers had to ship their products at premium rates and had several customer complaints. Our quality people recalled several items, reworked the product to rid it of noted defects and reshipped the product again. I did not have such problems as I made certain my requirements were built to the print established by our product engineering group. Besides, the process of recall and reworking a product is tremendously expensive. My work efforts and consistently completed assignments under some of the pressing circumstances were commended by my superiors, especially Dwayne, who closely monitored my performance within the organization.

Dwayne was another executive who expected a lot of his subordinates. He was college educated with a degree in engineering and several years of analytical engineering application in the manufacturing industry. He was also very effective in his ability to provide direction. He possessed a tremendous depth of manufacturing knowledge and understanding.

I was chosen by Dwayne, as well as other staff members, to work on special assignments and develop feasibility studies in order to enhance the efficiency of a given operation and ensure an economically favorable impact of the processes. I demonstrated superior work performance in those assignments and was recommended for other positions in the company. My recommendations provided the company with solutions to several of their most imminent problems regarding operations, resulting in rather substantial economic benefits.

It appeared on the surface that I had established a good working relationship with almost everyone at the facility, which consisted of thousands of workers. As time went on, several workers demonstrated their loyalty to me through the quality of work they performed.

As a manager, I became close to several of the people in the company as if they were family, since I spent most of my time at the company anyway. The workers often shared some of their most personal concerns with me. I heard of sicknesses and personal tragedy surrounding some of my workers and associates. Some people died of injury, heart attacks and other occurrences.

On occasion, when I returned to Wisconsin during the holidays (I often travelled back to the New York area for visits with family and friends or other activities), I was informed by co-workers of the tragedy of one worker who, for undisclosed reasons, had killed his wife, child and himself without any clear motive offered by those who knew him closely.

I remembered seeing the young man in the plant on several occasions and, although he did not work for me directly or indirectly, he often spoke to me as I passed him in the plant. He was always working during my presence, without a trace of any significant difficulty. The local newspapers in town did not provide all the details involved and after a few days there was not a lot of discussion about the tragic incident. Shortly thereafter, things went on as usual, and eventually this tragedy was forgotten.

In many instances, hourly workers are provided an opportunity to advance into management if they can show they have the necessary qualifications and potential to handle the duties of the position. Here, they are exposed to highly sensitive information regarding management operations, but still, their association and loyalty lie with the hourly group that provided them with their longest orientation. They continue to see their management co-workers as just that—management—and although a part of management now, they remain close to their Union comrades.

On many occasions, some of the hourly workers had access to operationally sensitive information before many of the management executives. This was not uncommon at GM. In addition, several high level corporate executives maintained their relationships with the line group of workers in order to continue the flow of information needed from the bottom of the company to the very top of it.

I took the nature of our business very seriously. On another occasion, I was given special assignment of a task of the utmost importance to the company. I was given a crew of workers not belonging to the regular group of people I normally managed. I had a couple employees who refused to continue the assignment after being placed on notice for possible disciplinary action after failing to report back to their assigned work station in a timely manner. They were counseled and told that they would be formally disciplined subject to further discussion with their Union representatives. In the presence of their representative, I personally escorted them from the plant, subject to my position in conjunction with labor relations, and considered their termination of employment. In consideration of the Union's involvement, the employees wished to be spared from termination of their jobs. Since this was their first offense, and it was secured by a promise that they never repeat their actions, the incident was reduced to time off and a written warning of record. Over time, these employees proved to be very good workers for me. The special assignment operation was successful as we completed a critical schedule ahead of time, still maintaining a high standard of quality.

After working in several areas of the plant in the manufacturing organization, I was chosen to work several additional special assignments and conduct analytical studies as needed. I welcomed the assignments with great enthusiasm. I thoroughly evaluated how the process worked and proposed ways to make it more efficient. I had the ability to resolve operational problems quickly and effectively. Later, I was flown to Divisional Headquarters in Michigan to have additional discussions with several corporate directors, mainly from financial and manufacturing operations. They, too, were impressed with my ability to discern myself with their particular operations and respond appropriately to the issues as they were presented.

When I returned from Divisional Headquarters, I was given additional assignments, participated in problem solving exercises and was appointed Manufacturing Budget Analyst in the financial organization of the company—a challenge I welcomed.

*   *   *

Although we worked religiously for the company throughout the day, after work several executives would meet at various establishments nearby our work facility. Some of the places were rather elegant and somewhat exclusive by some standards, but they were not a Waldorf, Americana, Hyatt or Hilton, as I had become accustomed to. We participated to enhance the acceptance and loyalty of our employees.

On a few occasions, some managers encountered hostile confrontations with disgruntled workers who may have had too much to drink. Several of these encounters were potentially explosive, with strong feelings on both sides. Other managers have given accounts of company executives who were involved in actual physical brawls with their employees at some of these gatherings. They had been ganged up on and beaten at times.

In order to get away from the frustrations of executive responsibility and day to day matters, many drank alcohol excessively. Both executive managers and hourly workers were involved in consuming large quantities of alcohol, both the evening before or during their breaks, and returning to work without a trace of having done so. They carried themselves very well and continued in many instances to operate their areas effectively.

I personally was not one of the executive managers of the company to drink as such. However, to be accepted by the other members of the team, I would periodically order a beer as well as pay for a round or more for those present. This activity was never held against them by me or anyone else to my knowledge. In fact, I had accepted them for who they were, as a part of my executive team back at the plant, and not for their activities outside of the company.

Many of us participated in other activities together, such as playing golf, fishing, bowling and attending football, baseball and basketball games. We frequented many of the familiar golf courses and country clubs. We generally fished in Lake Michigan from a chartered boat or pier. Lake Michigan is aesthetically beautiful throughout the year and is one of America's finest Great Lakes. Several individuals went game hunting for deer in Northern Wisconsin, where angry protests are still conducted by those who do not accept the Flambeau Indians' treaty entitlements established in the mid-1800s regarding certain fishing and land rights. Others went to Alaska or Utah to hunt grizzly bear and mountain lion during the hunting season. In this part of the country, almost everyone has a weapon since they are very easy to purchase—the wild, wild West, so to speak.

Many of these activities alleviated the stress of fulfilling one's responsibilities in a business environment filled with tremendous thundering noises from the heavy automated machinery. We required workers to wear hearing protection so they would not lose their hearing. Golfing and fishing proved to be the most tranquil in providing rejuvenation, especially for those who were occasionally frustrated for having to work in this kind of environment.

When casting a line into the deep waters of Lake Michigan several miles away from the shore to catch a limit of five brown trout or chinook salmon, you can see clearly through the bluish-green waters. In many instances, the prey approaches your line with such vigor the bait is removed very quickly. Further out you can see the skyline meet the plateau of the water's edge as the clouds complement the sky to provide a breath of fresh air. Conversation among the executives who attended the outings centered around sporting events. Whether it was football, baseball, basketball or hockey, or even what movies should be seen, there was always a subject that provided something of interest to talk about. On other occasions, several of us watched scheduled championship bouts. We also attended cookouts and family gatherings, as well as outings and events provided by the company. (At times, some of these scheduled activities were cancelled due to inclement weather or the imminent possibility of a tornado or blizzard, the likes of which are commonplace in the northern Midwest.)

The climate did not always permit us to enjoy the natural charm of the area. In fact, during the winter months, it was common to find yourself shoveling snow quite often. On a noted occasion, a Midwestern state received as much as 42 inches of snow, effectively shutting down its economy. In some instances following a heavy snowfall, I found myself shoveling around my residence three or four times a day, maybe five. When I reported to work during a heavy snowfall, the plant usually was at only 15-25% of operating capacity due to a high incidence of absenteeism. However, this occurred only a few times during the year because of hazardous road conditions or other complications associated with adverse weather. Quite often, the same people would show up for work and not take advantage of the situation, including myself. However, the conditions on those occasions were rather difficult and perhaps warranted their absence. Several of the workers always showed up to make certain the business was in order.

*   *   *

Proving my case against GM would have been a challenge for William Webster, former Director of the Federal Bureau of Investigation, and most recently Director of the Central Intelligence Agency. It is one of the greatest challenges of the decade.

Subsequent to the results of my first round of trials with the giant General Motors Corporation in State Court, I concluded the immediate audience at General Motors that was close to what had occurred to me had not been given a clear message to deter it from happening again. I believe I was correct and you will become privileged to it while reading the chronicles of this book.

While being subjected to the harassment and disrespect from Gil, Denis and their affiliates, I thought to myself that they were either suicidal, expendable, or limited in their careers, as I had grown angered by the adverse treatment I was experiencing. However, I caught myself and decided it was not proper for me to react and respond unprofessionally.

That evening as I returned home from work, I was very irritable and uneasy. I thought endlessly about why I was being treated that way. For the life of me, I could not understand what was going on. I had always completed my assignments on time or ahead of schedule. However, I continued to feel nauseous and light-headed, as if I were dizzy. When I would lie down, the feelings of wandering and dizziness would subside. When I would stand, my blood seemed to elevate, causing a spinning and wandering feeling, as if I were on speed or PCP. Of course, I have never taken drugs, nor had I felt dizziness in the past.

My wife saw my condition, and to ease my tension asked if I wanted to go out for dinner to take my mind off what had occurred at work. I said, "Sure. Let's go out."

We went to a local neighborhood Italian restaurant only to see one of the Union representatives there. His name was John.

My wife ordered the usual veal parmesan entrees for both of us and a large pizza for our oldest daughter. During that evening the light-headedness, dizziness and nauseous feeling came and went. I could not understand what was happening to me. The condition continued to vacillate for 30 or 45 minutes. It was an extremely unusual feeling. A more severe episode had occurred at work where it appeared as if I were having some kind of diabetic reaction. The occurrence at work was rather significant, and I wondered again why no one called for medical assistance. Why would they allow me to remain in that condition and leave the plant to return home?

This was the first and only time in my life I ever experienced that sort of reaction. I felt somewhat nauseous after drinking my usual cup of coffee. I always left it to cool, then walked away.

I began to realize someone wanted me out of the way completely, but the reason was unclear to me. I knew for one that Gil and Greg both felt uncomfortable about my qualifications and presence in the financial area. Gil is approximately 13 years older than me, and Greg is approximately three years older. Again, I was the youngest executive in my financial group during the time of the adverse treatment. I was responsible for several internal and external audits and was as objective and unyielding as they come, operating in the best interest of General Motors Corporation.

An adverse relationship had existed between Gil, Greg and myself since the beginning of the second week I was assigned to the financial area following my departure from manufacturing. Hence, the most important thing for me to do was to complete my work at the highest quality for the company, learning as much as I could. The comptroller, Joe, who supervised both Gil and myself, indicated to me that he did not agree with what Gil said in my appraisal. Gil rated my performance as needing improvement and better competence over all. This was entirely inconsistent with what I was actually doing. I had completed the assignments that were given to me each time with very little assistance, if any, from Gil. If given the proper appraisal from Gil, my salary would have gone up. He had complained about this shortly after I was assigned to his department. Therefore, giving me a bad or negative appraisal would keep my wages down.

He told me he had discussed my appraisal with Gil and asked him why he rated me the way he did. He said he did not see my performance as Gil did; he expressed that I had done a very good job as far as he was concerned.

Throughout the evening I continued to feel very uncomfortable and ill. I could not sleep at all during the entire weekend. I could not even focus my attention on the basketball game and other sports activities. It seemed as if no one realized what I was going through. I began to engage in long distance conversations with my relatives back East telling them what was happening to me. I even called doctors there and told them of my condition. I felt someone had tried to poison me, but it had not completely worked. However, by trying to diagnose my own condition by feeling and enduring it without medical assistance, my condition was growing worse. I continued to believe someone had poisoned me, and I would not accept that it was solely stress alone or an emotional episode of some kind.

At approximately 11:00 p.m. on Sunday evening, February 22, 1981, I called a medical doctor out East and talked to him. He immediately told me to get medical assistance right away. I told him because of the way I was being treated at work by Gil and Greg (mainly Gil), I could not trust anyone here. Besides, almost everyone I knew was out East, and they knew me very well. They would be able to tell that something was very wrong, indeed. I must say that I was very skeptical by this time, especially because of the way I was being treated. I had gone to hospitals on two occasions during my assignment in the financial department of General Motors for severe nausea and other discomforts, and those physicians had questioned the kind of work I was doing. They said the work alone could cause my condition. However, I believed there was more to it than that. For the life of me, I could not understand why General Motors, Gil and his associates, would be treating an up-and-coming executive this way.

I knew Gil wanted my position for someone else, as it is a highly visible position. He knew I was intelligent and would learn the intricacies of GM on my own since I had already begun to show evidence of mastering the entire financial system.

It appeared as if a catalyst was added to completely destroy me, as the occurrence in some respects destroyed my reputation and credibility. I thought maybe there was something more to this, maybe someone was trying to poison me or slip me a hallucinogenic substance to cause disorientation and high levels of anxiety.

After speaking with Dr. Angel, a medical doctor out East, I tried calling Jim, another doctor I know. However, I could not reach him. Then I called my father. I told him to take the next plane to come get me because I was not feeling well. I told him I had become very nauseous at work, that the illness first occurred there and that somehow I was becoming disoriented and could not sleep. I said I could not trust anyone here because they had seen me at the General Motors office and allowed me to leave the plant in that condition. He said he would call me back. When he called me back he indicated he would fly in the next morning to get me. By this time it was about 11:45 p.m. on Sunday evening. I did not sleep for the entire evening. The next thing I knew, it was 5:30 a.m. By this time I had grown very exhausted. However, since I hardly took a day off, I wanted to go to work. I realized I was not in a condition or frame of mind to go to work.

On Monday morning, I called work and informed Gil I would not be coming in that day as I continued to feel ill. That morning I did not allow my wife to leave our apartment because I thought I was going to die. I knew there was nothing mentally wrong with me at all. I refused to accept that physically and mentally my body had given in, although I was told the adverse treatment I received on a weekly basis for two years in the financial organization at General Motors could cause what had occurred. I am not a medical expert, however; I can differentiate between certain feelings.

My neighbor indicated I appeared anxious on Friday evening, however, it was nothing like what occurred at the GM office that Saturday around mid-afternoon. It seemed as if Gil did everything he could during my assignment in the financial organization to destroy my career and undermine my powerful presence. Suddenly, it seemed my career at General Motors Corporation would be lost forever.

* * *

When my father arrived on Monday morning he appeared shocked to see me in such a terrible condition. He wanted to take me to a local hospital. I insisted he make arrangements to fly me out East for medical assistance. I did not want anyone to cover up or assist in my demise.

We made arrangements to fly the entire family back to the New York-New Jersey area. During our flight I periodically continued to feel very light-headed and dizzy, as if I were suddenly on the verge of blacking out. The plane had a stop in Detroit, Michigan, of all places, and several middle-aged executives stepped onto the plane. Two of them stared at me with what seemed like endless concern.

I tried to recollect who they were but could not remember. Throughout the flight I continued thinking silently to myself trying to reason why this was happening. Why was I being treated this way by those in the financial organization and by Denis Cronk, who said the company had conducted an investigation. He said, "You are not who you said you were; you're a phony." He began to attack my educational credentials. I told him he was seriously mistaken.

It was difficult for me to tell if all this was well orchestrated by the enormous General Motors organization, or if it was just a group of executives who desired my elimination because of something I had seen or learned after I had begun to examine highly detailed and sensitive information. My mind was substantially opened due to my analytical responsibilities, and somehow these executives knew it. They began fabricating uncertainty, doubt and disbelief. I was persecuted as if I were the subject of investigation by the CIA.

As our plane arrived in Newark Airport, I first felt relieved, but about 25 minutes later I felt dizzy and light-headed again.

Soon I was greeted by my immediate family members and some friends. They were shocked to see me in that condition. We went down to the lower level of the airport to get our baggage from the carousel. By this time I had grown very hungry. I did not want my condition to grow worse, as I suspected something was not right here; it had to be something more than just an anxiety attack.

During the drive from the airport, I had normal conversation with my relatives and friends. Then, I experienced another episode of disorientation, almost to the point of blacking out, accompanied by dizziness.

When I arrived at my mother's home in New Jersey, my mother was terrified by my condition. I contacted one of my best friends, Joe, whom I had known as a child. I asked that he come over and take me to a hospital. When he saw me he could not believe my condition either. I was completely exhausted. He stated very concerned, "Gary, what did they do to you?"

I said, "I'm not sure, completely, Joe."

He said, "I'm taking you to see Dr. Angel."

We notified Dr. Angel I would meet him in the emergency room of the hospital. It was approximately 9:45 p.m. Monday evening when my wife, Joe and I arrived at the hospital. Dr. Angel arrived approximately 30 minutes later. He was astonished to see me so exhausted and anxious. He questioned me extensively about reality and my presence, as most experts would. I survived his reality test. I was not talking to myself, nor was I out of touch with reality. I explained to him what was happening to me during my two-year assignment at General Motors and what had happened the final Saturday at work which caused me additional anxiety. The doctor took my blood pressure, examined the pupils of my eyes and took my pulse. I could see the fear and concern in his eyes and facial expression.

He appeared very angry for he knew what occurred to me was not ordinary. My condition was deliberately brought on by the conditions surrounding my work at General Motors Corporation.

Throughout the entire interview, Dr. Angel seemed very concerned about my condition as his non-verbal and verbal expressions indicated.

He said, "Jesus, what have they done to you?"

I said, "I'm not sure, since I don't drink, smoke or take any drugs. I don't know."

He further stated, "You are completely exhausted; your affect has caused you to worry." Then he stated very loudly, "Gary, what about your career? Do you realize that with your present condition, your career may be substantially damaged and lost forever?"

I said, "I know, Dr. Angel. I have to get back to work immediately. I've committed so much time to my educational and professional development." In addition, I said, "You know I have to get back to the area because I only have three more credits to complete my Master's degree at the University of Wisconsin."

The mere fact that I had gone back to graduate school at the University of Wisconsin to complete my degree in taxation caused some individuals in my financial group to resent me. Suddenly, I experienced this mysterious condition two months before I was scheduled to complete my graduate training.

I did, however, receive good grades in the two courses I was taking. School has always been a comfort zone for me. I received positive feedback there as opposed to the unwarranted mental stress heaped on me by Denis and the financial group at GM. If I had not gone back to school, I probably would have had this occurrence sooner. I received high marks in graduate school in spite of the frustrations I received at work.

I asked Gil to send me to the General Motors Training Institute for a couple weeks for the Advanced Financial Analysis course offered by the company. Gil vehemently denied me the opportunity to receive this training. The course would have provided me with additional knowledge and insights into the financial necessities of the huge automotive company, but Gil, Greg and Denis limited my development and tried to neutralize my interest and motivation.

Dr. Angel provided me with a choice of medication—injections or pills. I selected pill form and he ordered neuroleptics (tranquilizers) and counseled me for about an hour. He asked me if I felt comfortable at my mother's home or if I would prefer to stay in the hospital for a couple days. I chose my mother's home.

He called the night shift nurse into the room, ordered the medication, and suggested I take it, since it would alleviate my anxiety. He completely ruled out the presence of any psychosis. It was strictly a heightened state of anxiousness. He prescribed the medication, suggested several days of bed rest and asked to check me medically twice a week to monitor my progress and adjust the medication, as necessary.

When I left the hospital with my wife and Joe, I felt the medication begin to take affect. I suddenly felt extremely tired and drowsy as I walked down the street. I looked to my right and saw a crowd gather outside a funeral home. I saw a bright light shining in the window where the body was laid and services were held. I thought to myself it could have been me if I had waited any longer to ask for medical assistance. However, for the life of me, I could not understand why Gil and the others would allow me to walk out of the GM facility in that condition without offering to call for medical assistance. What was going on there? What did they not want me to see and why were they trying to lessen my credibility at the giant automotive company? I had conducted myself very professionally and completed my assignments objectively and in the best interest of the company.

I concluded that management operated irresponsibly regarding my condition. As a manager of Union workers, I was required to offer and provide such medical assistance to those workers. If I failed to provide aid to an injured worker, or any Union worker who had an occurrence similar to mine, more than likely a Union representative would file a grievance against me for failing to do so. In fact, the Union would probably recommend my termination. To the best of my knowledge, nothing happened to Gil or Denis, because by this time they had aligned themselves with higher authority. My position had been made available to the executive the higher authority wanted to accommodate, regardless of my qualifications and contribution to the company. Obviously, there were additional individuals who possessed more power than Gil. This became evident to me as Gil and Denis became more aggressive toward me. Their objective was to neutralize and, if possible, completely destroy any power affiliations with other high ranking executives by casting a shadow of doubt on my loyalty with the company. This character assassination through the process of giving me negative performance reviews, regardless of what I had accomplished, would prove I was expendable.

During this involvement with Gil and Denis, I recalled that even before I was assigned to work with them in the financial area, and after just having brief encounters with them in passing at the General Motors facility, they were rather unpleasant compared to the many managers I did come in contact with. There was very strong talk that I was going to be considered unclassified over a short duration, and I was approximately 13 years younger than Gil and 15 years younger than Denis.

After the first night of full rest which, without question, was brought on by the neuroleptics given to me by Dr. Angel, I was able to relax. I was not agitated nor was I overly concerned about my health. Although I knew something of a very traumatic nature had happened to me, I was still uncertain as to why I was treated that way. I did not see anyone else treated in that manner, even executives at the company who did not have similar outstanding performance ratings as did I and who performed different work assignments.

The very next morning, I heard my wife and mother talking in the dining room of my mother's home about the details of my situation. I got out of bed at approximately 8:00 a.m. It had been the first full night of sleep I received in quite some time. As I stepped out of the guest room, I saw happy expressions grow on the faces of my mother and my wife.

We engaged in extensive conversation regarding how I felt and what my plans were. I immediately directed my wife to call Joe, the comptroller in charge of the General Motors financial area at the facility and notify him that I was in New Jersey and I would be taking a medical leave of absence for several weeks, as recommended by Dr. Angel. I then contacted my real estate attorney, in whom I had a lot of trust and confidence. I thought it would be good for me to inform someone of his stature about my condition in the event there were complications I would not survive.

When Paul, the attorney, arrived I appeared relaxed in casual attire. I had been heavily sedated the night before, which contributed to my somewhat sluggish appearance. However, I was still sharp in many respects, including my ability to reason and make meaningful decisions.

He expressed concern about what had happened to me and offered suggestions about getting a second medical opinion, given the adverse treatment I had been subjected to. During the course of this conversation, my father arrived. He was upset I was not resting and had been conducting business as usual with my attorney. My father, more or less, was reacting to the condition that he had seen me in and how I had been treated. He angrily insisted that Paul not ask me any additional questions about my medical condition or what had happened. I assertively said to my father, "Al, it's okay. Paul is concerned about the circumstances surrounding my condition and what happened." Paul indicated to my father that he was only trying to help.

Suddenly my conversation with Paul and my father was interrupted as my wife called out to me, "Gary, I've contacted Joe, the comptroller. He's on the phone now!"

I could hear her yelling at Joe, "What did you people do to my husband? What did you do to Gary?"

I immediately interrupted the conversation and said, "Shirley, stop, stop. Don't talk to Joe that way. Joe is okay. He has not done anything to me directly. He's okay. Don't talk to him that way. Keep the conversation simple with him. Just inform him that I'll be on medical leave from the company for several weeks, as recommended by my doctor." I continued, "Calm down, Shirley. Let me handle this my way. I want to collect additional information regarding the events as they occurred. Joe has not caused any direct harm to me, as did Gil and Denis. Those are the ones I want, and I will develop a plan to resolve this entire matter as they developed their plan to destroy my career and blemish the reputation I worked so hard to establish."

My wife was able to regain her composure and resumed talking to Joe, who was in his Wisconsin office at GM. She informed him I would be taking the time off. He indicated to her that he hoped I would get better and sent his regards to me.

I said, "Now that's taken care of. I don't want to jeopardize my position and benefits with the company for failing to report to work as scheduled." I then told my wife we would have to make arrangements to put my daughter in private school. We contacted several schools in the area and finally selected Our Lady of Mercy, close to our home in New Jersey.

After taking care of several important concerns, I rejoined Paul and my father in the living room. Paul and I continued our conversation. He later said if I wanted a second opinion to contact him since he knew a very good physician who could discuss what had occurred. I told him, "Thanks, but I think I have a very good understanding of what happened." I personally concluded that what happened to me would have happened to anyone who possessed my education and qualifications. These people appeared to be more concerned about my presence than my development as an outstanding corporate executive at GM, as I had been rated before working with Gil and Denis.

It seemed as if they were trying to deliberately and permanently damage a diamond in the rough. I made certain to deliver high quality work and completed it on schedule. The work was not difficult for me at all, and again I was the only employee during this time with the educational qualifications in this particular area. However, I did not think my presence or qualifications would incite them to subject me to adverse conditions and cause the kind of injury I had experienced.

On several occasions, Greg said he was not going to show anyone of my stature anything regarding his position or anything that would give them more understanding. I asked why. He said he had been overlooked for a promotion previously and the person he helped had received it. I asked why that bothered him and said, "Eventually you will get your promotion."

He said, "Yeah, but this person was promoted two levels, and he wasn't as knowledgeable as you are."

At this point, I knew Gil and Greg were very concerned about the level to which I would advance if they allowed my career to go smoothly and without incidence of adverse treatment.

Paul left around 12:30 p.m., saying, "Call me if you need me, and I'll call again to stay in touch."

I said, "Okay. Thanks."

My wife brought me my medication as prescribed. I took the medicine and it completely overwhelmed me, as I could not keep my eyes open. It made me sleep once again. After sleeping each time I would feel better and stronger. Before my assignment to the financial organization at General Motors Corporation, I always felt strong and healthy.

Later on during the week several other friends and relatives stopped in to visit me. I continued to visit Dr. Angel about twice a week for physical examination and medication adjustment. Dr. Angel indicated it was very important that I take the medicine since it allowed me to sleep and get rest, which was important to my complete recovery. He stated my condition had been brought on by my employment. He also said ordinary work responsibilities could have caused my condition, but also acknowledged that I was subjected to adverse conditions and had lost so much sleep that my REM sleep had been substantially disturbed. Sleep loss can be brought on by several factors: stress, caffeine, PCP, anxiety and a host of others. Once the cause is identified, one can eliminate the disorder. Sleep deprivation produces anxiety, disorientation and a host of other problems. I told Dr. Angel I felt someone had drugged me or poisoned me and that was why I had to return.

Dr. Angel indicated I was fortunate to have survived the seriousness of my affliction. I was angry that this seemed to have been conducted deliberately against me to prevent me from completing the remaining three credits of my Master's degree and destroy my GM career completely. Everyone around me sensed I was on my way to the top, and knew I was one of the youngest managers to do this. However, someone did not want it to happen.

I began to think back on who was around my desk. I remembered that Greg sat next to me, John was in front of me and Paul, a maintenance superintendent, sat at my desk in January and on a couple of other occasions during a financial investigation regarding his department. Later, he was offered early retirement.

I received a phone call from Wilbert, a very close management associate. He wanted to know how I was doing. He further stated what happened to me was well-publicized throughout the plant and that several people could not understand why they would do that to me. He also said John, who was in the accounting area on that Saturday, came down to the quality lab and told Bill I must have been drugged because of my reaction. He asked Bill if he were aware of me taking any kind of drugs.

Bill responded, "Are you kidding? Gary does not take drugs. He would barely drink a beer."

The medical department divulged confidential medical information. Instead of saying I was treated for stress and a sleep disorder, they said I was treated for mental anxiety to further damage my reputation at the General Motors plant. Someone was definitely trying to destroy my image and reputation. I asked Wilbert, "How did John know I felt as if someone had drugged or poisoned me?" although I had been under an unusual amount of stress to begin with.

On May 4, 1981, I returned to work at the General Motors facility in Wisconsin. As soon as I returned I was approached by Bonnie from Personnel who immediately stated, "If I were you I would be concerned about my career. I would . . . would be asking some people some questions about what this is going to do to my career." I was given several internal and external audit assignments and other financial statistical assignments. I efficiently and accurately completed all assignments with the utmost precision and quality. I continued to run the manufacturing information center and computer printouts. I encountered Denis who briefly said he was sorry to be involved in causing me injury, but that if I took it to court he would deny it.

The giant automotive company was experiencing sharp declines in their car sales because of the economy and fierce competition coming from abroad, mainly from Japan. The company had to make adjustments to its staff and select people for layoff. Since I had greater plant seniority and a higher assignment level, I would not be affected.

When a couple of Gil's friends were chosen for layoff, he continued to be difficult in his relationship with me. He never provided me with the kind of direction a manager should. I feel qualified to make this statement because I was also a manager and had received the highest ratings the company had to offer. I could not understand why Gil was not as effective in providing the same kind of management and treatment.

Later Greg said again that the company was changing its policy regarding retention and layoff consideration from seniority to performance. He said, "If I were you, I would be concerned."

I said, "Why should I be concerned? My seniority has survived the guidelines for those requirements."

He said, "It doesn't matter."

I said, "Well, I complete all my assignments without any difficulty and with good quality."

He said, "Well, Gil said he was going to give you a lower rating."

When I asked why, he said, "Because he doesn't like you."

I said, "That's nothing new. I've known that from the beginning, but I do all my work for the company. I cannot change the way he feels about me. I am a businessman."

A couple months later I was selected by Gil for layoff regardless of my seniority. In December, I was summoned into Joe's office, and he reluctantly informed me of the situation. I conducted myself very professionally and departed the company office facilities later that day when my shift ended.

One week later, on December 18, 1981, I went to an agency of the Department of Labor and Industry to file my very first charge against the General Motors Corporation regarding all conditions of employment I was subjected to there. I knew Wisconsin was a rather conservative state, but my decision was made after providing GM with ample opportunity to settle this matter internally.

After putting aside my most immediate concerns, I decided to organize factual material and assertions for presentation to the labor officials. The initial complaint I brought to the Department of Labor and Industry was rather extensive and included the facts and events leading to what I experienced with GM at the hands of their designated executives. The case was prepared solely by me. I interviewed several attorneys to help me resolve the issues between GM and myself. An attorney whom I did not know referred me to one, Mark, in early 1982. In June of that year, Mark confirmed he would represent my case.

During this time, I received several phone calls from other management executives who expressed their disbelief and concern regarding my layoff, which was inappropriate and in clear violation of proper procedures. I knew that eventually, after several inappropriate and inaccurate criticisms of my work, Gil would ultimately harm my career with the corporation. I sensed this from the very beginning when I had my first brief encounter with him regarding my expenses for relocation. When I was given the financial assignment from the manufacturing organization, I was not too concerned about Gil's presence as I knew that not only was I an outstanding worker, but also a very hard worker who had an endless drive to complete all assignments with exceptional quality. Besides, I thought as long as I completed all assignments with professionalism, Gil's presence would not be much of a concern for me.

I began to realize there seemed to be a conspiracy to lessen my image in the eyes of other managers who had a high regard for me and the work I performed. I made numerous requests internally to General Motors staff executives and others to make immediate arrangements to have me transferred from the financial organization in Wisconsin to another division of General Motors Corporation or back to the New York metropolitan area, in an effort to protect my career. I indicated there was nothing difficult about the work, however, it was Gil and one of his affiliates who provided additional unnecessary burdens for me to contend with.

Personally, I was well liked and admired by a substantial number of individuals at GM. The encounters I experienced with Gil and Denis were unfamiliar to me. I had never experienced this kind of treatment or attitude from previous employers. I knew my employment rights were being violated and I was being treated unfairly.

The only reason I made the request to transfer to the New York-New Jersey area was to get past the attitudes of Gil and Denis and save my career.

However, it seemed as if someone were sabotaging my career by programming me to fail and creating a negative mindset in those who had immediate interaction with me.

In retrospect, while developing important information to provide to the Department of Labor and Industry, I realized I would not only be protecting my employment rights, but would also be considered disloyal to the giant automotive company and would engage in an extremely difficult and complicated fight with this powerful, influential organization. This involvement would change me forever. Nevertheless, I realized I had been substantially damaged, and I was determined to use every available alternative to be restored.

*   *   *

As soon as I received the phone call from Bonnie, informing me I would be called back from layoff and was required to report back to work that Monday morning at 8:00 a.m., I immediately said to my wife, "You know, I think they are calling me back because of the charge I filed with the Labor Department."

My wife said, "Do you think that's the only reason?"

I said, "Yes. If you examine their actions closely, you will see their decision to call me back was made shortly after they were notified by the Labor Department." At this point it was unclear if they wanted me to report back to work to resolve this matter or to continue working as I had in the past. "However," I said, "Whatever their rationale is, I will report to work on Monday as they request so I don't forfeit any of my entitlements or violate the company's employment guidelines."

My wife said, "Well, don't you think they'll be angry with you for filing the charge with the Labor Department? Aren't you concerned about what's going to happen?"

"Certainly, but if you're talking about how they're going to feel about what I did, the answer is no. I'm not concerned that the company stood behind Gil and allowed him to affect my position by giving me lower performance ratings and choosing me for layoff clearly in violation of my seniority and company guidelines at that time. However, I am concerned about how this will ultimately affect my career at General Motors and elsewhere. I suspect General Motors will retaliate against me for bringing such a charge before the Labor Department. They must be anticipating a lawsuit being filed against them. Personally, Shirley, I think since General Motors and their representatives have had ample time to prepare themselves after reviewing the charge before the Labor Department, that they had no other choice than to bring me back, because they are clearly in violation of my employment entitlements. That's important to any worker in the United States of America. This is not a communist country; you need your job to survive financially."

It appeared as if a member of the Union had more employment protection recognized and abided by General Motors Corporation than their salaried executive personnel.

As I continued my conversation with my wife, I said, "You know, General Motors would have to bring me back so they'd be able to completely change all my appraisals in an attempt to develop documentation of poor job performance and neutralize any intentions I may have in taking them to court if the Labor Department cannot get them to resolve my concerns."

"Why do you think they would do something like that?" my wife asked.

"So they wouldn't be defeated in court."

"Do you think it will go that far? Will you have to take it to court?" my wife asked.

"Why, certainly," I said. "I do not honestly think General Motors is concerned with contending with representatives from the Labor Department against their attorneys. General Motors is not intimidated with this process at all. In fact, they are rather used to legal proceedings and could quickly end a case before it gets before a jury. At this stage, I think it is too early for me to concern myself with what they may or may not do, but I must concern myself with reporting back to work and doing an exceptional job, better than what I did previously. Now I am considered an adversary and anything I do wrong will be documented and held against me."

When I returned to work at the General Motors facility, I was greeted by several managers with whom I previously worked. They appeared happy to see I was back at work once more. For the folks in Personnel, it seemed business as usual.

I was immediately summoned to the Personnel Offices of the company. Tom and Bonnie welcomed me back to work. We had a brief discussion about how things were being conducted and how pleased they were to see I was returning to work.

Several hours passed and I was still waiting for my assignment. As I sat and waited for the personnel indoctrination process to end, I saw Denis quickly pass the administrative offices, glancing in my direction. He continued his travels to another location of the building. Gil did not appear during my presence in the waiting area of Personnel.

Bonnie came out of an office with Tom, the Assistant Personnel Manager under Phil. There were two other gentlemen unknown to me standing in Tom's office engaged in conversation with Tom. Bonnie had several documents with him when he came out of Tom's office.

As I waited for further instruction at the General Motors office, Bonnie began walking in my direction with several documents in his hand. He made an about face and went back into Tom's office with the two other gentlemen I did not know. He engaged in brief conversation with Tom and the two men and soon began his approach in my direction. I was not privileged to the conversation behind closed doors. The company usually has an "open door" policy to discuss administrative concerns, but this policy was not made available to me at this time. In fact, it appeared as if this entire policy was used so the company could gain insight into what my problem entailed and how they could defend against it if they had to.

Bonnie was a salaried worker who handled labor problems. As Bonnie approached me, he asked me to come into an office next to the waiting area to discuss the company plans regarding my return to work. He indicated to me that the company had been notified by the Department of Labor and Industry and had several concerns surrounding my selection for layoff from the General Motors facility. He stated that the company officials were upset and concerned about my complaint and the charges against them. They wanted to completely resolve this matter now, and that had been his reason for contacting me last Thursday evening regarding the need for me to report to work. "The company requires you to sign a release," he said. "It releases all legal claims you may have now or in the future regarding the charges and complaint filed before the Labor Department."

I said, "Bonnie, you have to be kidding."

He said, "I am not. This is serious. The company made an agreement with the Labor Department to bring you back to work if you sign a release and drop all liabilities against the company."

"Bonnie, no one from the Labor Department contacted me and informed me of any settlement of this or any other kind." I continued, "This is no way to resolve my concerns with the company. If you want to effectively set aside and resolve my concerns, then I suggest everyone go over all the details and issues in a formal meeting. I will not, absolutely not, sign anything you or anyone else brings before me. If you want me to return to work, to work, I could oblige you in that regard. Bonnie, I want you to understand. The issues before you and the company are important to me, and unless they are handled properly, I will not sign anything until they are settled. If you do not want me to continue working for the company, then say so."

"Gary, you have to sign the release or you won't have a position with the company, more or less," Bonnie said.

"I understand what your requirements are, however, I am not prepared to sign, and I will not sign, any release at this time. It's rather premature to do so, and you have not come to me with any meaningful plan of resolution."

"Then Gary, I don't know what's going to happen to you with the company."

"What do you mean, Bonnie?"

"I mean I don't know what the company will do with you."

"Are you saying the only reason you called me back without my personal representatives present was to somehow get me to sign a release stating I would not have any claims against the company?"

"I didn't say the only reason we called you back was to get you to sign the release, but it is a requirement for you to return to work."

"Bonnie, listen to me. If you haven't heard anything I have said to you during our conversation, then hear this. For the last time, I'm telling you I will not sign a release of any kind until all my requirements, as stipulated before the Labor Department are reasonably satisfied. Now, I hope you understand fully what my requirements are. I want you to go back to your committee and ask them to fully review all my demands and see if we can come to some kind of resolution. In addition, since I was wrongfully placed on layoff clearly as an infringement to my seniority status, if you want me to remain in this status of layoff, then let me know. Since I've told you I will not sign any documents as a condition for me to return to work, I have only two questions for you. Should I go? Or should I stay?"

Bonnie appeared baffled and flustered. He knew I had already made up my mind on the day I was wrongfully selected for layoff in clear violation of my employment entitlements that I would do whatever was necessary, including significant litigation, to recover those entitlements wrongfully taken from me.

Bonnie responded after several moments of silence, "I don't know."

I said, "Well, if you don't, who does?"

He responded, "Hold on, Gary. I'll be back in a moment."

Bonnie left the office momentarily. From where I was sitting I could see he had gone into another office four offices from where I was. It apparently was that of Tom, the Assistant Personnel Manager. Phil, who was in charge of Personnel, was out of town.

As I got up from my seat in the office where Bonnie and I had our discussion, I could see Tom was on the phone and Bonnie was talking directly to him. They both had very serious expressions on their faces, as if something very tragic had occurred. Approximately 15 minutes passed. Tom and Bonnie were still engaged in conversation, and they appeared to both be looking out the window near the main entrance at the General Motors facility.

The two gentlemen who were in Tom's office earlier were not present now. As Bonnie and Tom continued their conversation, I approached Tom's secretary and asked if they would be long. Nancy responded, "Gary, I don't know how long they'll be. Tom just received an outside call and he's in conference.

Tom did not appear to be talking on the phone; however, I did notice a conference call box near his window. Apparently Tom and Bonnie were having a conference call with people outside the plant. I went back to the waiting area of the office.

Several colleagues of mine welcomed me back to work as I stood waiting for Bonnie to let me know what the company had decided about my return to work and my direct refusal to sign any kind of document. Approximately one hour and several minutes passed before Bonnie appeared from Tom's office.

Finally, I saw Bonnie come out of Tom's office for a brief moment. He stopped only to go back into Tom's office again where he engaged in additional conversation. Tom picked up the telephone again. Ten more minutes went by. Tom and Bonnie continued conversation as Tom hung up the phone. Bonnie looked as if he were seriously concerned about something, as did Tom. Suddenly, Bonnie appeared again. As he approached me, he seemed annoyed. He called me into the office where we initially conducted our discussions regarding my return to work.

Bonnie said, "Gary, you know you are going about this the wrong way. According to corporate guidelines and my conversations with Linda from the Labor Department, you must . . ."

"Bonnie, excuse me for interrupting you, however, I simply need you to answer two questions. Should I stay? Or should I go?"

There was a brief moment of silence and Bonnie, after pondering annoyedly, said, "You are scheduled to report to Dave on second shift manufacturing this evening."

I said, "Is this my final assignment?"

Bonnie responded, "For now it is until I fully determine what the company is going to do."

I said, "Well, I am very cooperative, as you and the company know, and I'll be available to discuss with the company any questions they may have."

Bonnie stated, "Well, you know this is not the last time you will see me until this thing is resolved."

I said, "I am certain of that, but, for the record, I want you to know that it is not my position to disrespect or disobey the company's guidelines or policies. Hence, it is my position to make certain, formally or informally, that the company knows exactly what my position and concerns are."

Bonnie stated, "I am certain they know what your position is."

I stated, "Well then, they'll have to show me it is perfectly clear to them and that they intend to resolve a problem deliberately caused by someone else against me. Tell me why the company is bringing me back into a hostile environment where people are angry about what I've done? Why doesn't the company just transfer me?"

Bonnie stated, "If I were you, I'd be concerned about my career."

I said, "I am concerned about my career. That's why I filed the charge with the Labor Department to begin with . . . to get my job back or transfer from this GM facility to salvage my career. I want to avoid defamatory appraisals in the form of deliberate understatements of my true performance as were given in the accounting area by those who did not want my career to continue.

"As you can see, I have several concerns which cannot be resolved at this level, to protect my interest and that of General Motors."

Bonnie wanted to say something further, but I said, "Don't say anything else. I have to leave now so I can report back to work on the second shift operations, as you suggested."

I immediately left the General Motors facility, greeting several management executives as I walked through the corridors leading to the exit for the salaried personnel parking lot. I got into my car and drove to my residence. When I got home I greeted my wife who was tending to my youngest daughter; my oldest was attending school.

My wife said, "What happened? Why are you home?"

I said, "The company decided I will be going back to manufacturing and I have to report to second shift in about an hour."

Shirley said, "How come they kept you at work most of the day if you have to go back to work on second shift?"

I said, "All morning the company was trying to get me to sign a release document."

"What did you do?"

"I didn't sign it. I flatly refused to sign the release."

"What kind of release was it?"

"Well, it's a document releasing General Motors from any claims before the Labor Department and any legal claims I may bring outside of General Motors. Excuse me, Dear, for a moment. I only have a short while, and I must make a very important phone call."

"An important phone call?" my wife asked. "To whom?"

"To Linda at the Department of Labor and Industry. Listen, Hon, I can't explain now. I don't have a lot of time to talk to you about this, but I want you to understand. I have to go to work soon, and I have to get a hold of Linda before I do. I need to find out exactly what she said to General Motors representatives regarding my return to work. I cannot believe she would enter into any agreement with the company without my approval."

"Why do you think she did that?" my wife asked.

"Because Bonnie indicated he had discussions with Linda from the Department of Labor and Industry and that it was her understanding after talking with him that I was to sign a release in order to return to work. I must talk with Linda to confirm this. I think it's highly improper for someone to forsake my employment entitlements without my considerations being expressed. Shirley, excuse me. I have to make this call. I'm running out of time."

At this moment I quickly picked up the phone and dialed the Department of Labor and Industry. The phone was busy. I called again and again only to hear a busy signal. I became frustrated because I had to go back to work without any clear understanding of what was going to happen to my claims before the Labor Department.

I looked at the clock and noticed I had only 15 minutes left before I was required to leave for work. I told my wife that this discussion concerning my conditional return to work made me feel uncomfortable. I decided to take a shower, but first I tried to contact Linda again. Again, when I called I got a busy signal. On this day when I wanted to talk with someone at the Labor Department the most I simply could not get through.

I hurried into the shower to refresh myself and ease the frustration caused by my conference with General Motors representatives, mainly Bonnie, during this morning's meeting.

I said to my wife during my shower, "How can General Motors expect me to sign a release without formal discussions with them or without even consulting a lawyer regarding the issues before the Labor Department? What the hell do they take me for anyway? Here I am deliberately and mysteriously injured at work and harassed by Gil and Denis, causing damage to my corporate and professional reputation without reasonable cause.

"I provided General Motors, by their representatives, every conceivable means of resolving my concerns regarding their treatment of me through the company's open door policy which most often I found to have been actually closed to me and nothing is resolved."

As I stepped out of the shower, I picked up the phone and called the Labor Department; once more the line was busy.

I immediately dressed and secured my briefcase. As I began walking out the door, I turned once again, picked up the phone and called the Labor Department. Finally, the call went through. "May I speak to Linda?" I asked.

The voice responded, "Who's calling?"

"Mr. McKnight."

"I'm sorry. Linda is gone for the week."

"You're kidding?"

"No. She'll be in next Monday."

"Well, if she calls in, have her call me. It's rather urgent. I have to go now."

I slammed the phone down and said to my wife, "I can't believe this! What is going on? How can anyone negotiate my return to work without my consent? I simply cannot understand how anyone could take it upon themselves to make decisions about my concerns without discussing any kind of meaningful settlement with me."

"Maybe Linda was talking with General Motors management personnel to initiate talks regarding your concerns," Shirley said.

"I don't think so. Bonnie told me Linda said it would be necessary for me to sign a release in order to return to work. He cannot make the decision regarding my entitlements under the law in this manner.

"Then again, I can't believe what they are saying the Labor Department said because of the untruths regarding the performance rating I received which laid the groundwork for my layoff to begin with. Why should I believe General Motors' representatives about what the people from the Labor Department decided regarding my return to work? Shirley, you see, this is why it's necessary for the Labor Department to have a formal meeting regarding my concerns."

"I think you're right. It does seem rather strange that the Labor Department is not involved in your discussions with General Motors."

"When I go in to work this evening I have to be extremely careful with everything I do because General Motors management will be documenting it. You know that, don't you?"

"You think so?" Shirley replied.

"Of course. General Motors, in my opinion, is bringing me back for one reason . . . to attempt to destroy me in any way they can, but mainly to destroy the credibility of my management performance and ultimately to add further mindset."

"Why would they do that?"

"To strengthen their legal position against me if they ever had to go to court against me. Currently, the evidence regarding my performance and qualifications places them at a disadvantage. What I am saying is this: I am not flaunting my qualifications or my accomplishments, but several managers at GM may be jealous because I do have better qualifications than they have.

"General Motors, it seems, simply does not have an interest in developing me as an executive who would take charge of the company someday. I've found during my involvement in the financial area of the company they have a total disregard of my qualifications.

"You know, Shirley, it seems as if several managers are intimidated by my qualifications. I sensed this from the very beginning of my assignment to the financial area. That's why I hesitated to complete the remaining six credits of my Master's degree.

"Shirley, look back during the time I decided to complete the last six credits of my Master's degree. Two months before graduating, I had a mysterious accident at work. I was dizzy, had a feeling of tripping, and stomach pains which lead to a medical leave that interrupted the completion of my graduation requirements.

"I have never experienced such an attitude of resentment anywhere that I can recall. I don't understand how anyone could interfere intentionally with a person's career to the extent they have interfered with mine."

"Some people just want to do harm against others for many reasons, including jealousy," Shirley said.

"Why should they be resentful and jealous of me? Why?"

"Because you are very intelligent and handsome and, as you said before, very qualified," Shirley stated.

"I am simply working for the best interest of the company. I don't deserve to be exposed to anyone with that kind of attitude. My accomplishments and contributions to General Motors are documented."

"I know, Dear. You're way out of their league," my wife said.

"I don't like to think so, but you may be right. General Motors is not going to give me the opportunity to return to work to continue my professional development and advancement. They are simply bringing me back to change my performance appraisals and ultimately destroy my career. The Labor Department should know this."

"Maybe you shouldn't go in to work until you can get a hold of the Labor Department officials, if you think that's what they are going to do," Shirley said.

"Don't you see? I have to report to work or they'll say they offered to return me to work and I refused to accept it. If there were any further action in a court of law, potentially this could jeopardize my position. If I return to work, General Motors will develop a plan to render low performance appraisals and will fire me eventually, regardless of what I do."

"Why would they want to do that to you?" Shirley asked.

"First ask, 'Why did they do what they did to you in the first place?' I was subjected to all that harassment and abuse when I was working, without causing General Motors any problems. Besides, as a result of filing the charges with the Labor Department, General Motors management hates me. They see me as an outcast instead of a team player and will do whatever they can to destroy me. However, I simply don't give a damn at this point I'm going to do the best I can to continue doing an outstanding job for the company as I was hired to do, as my previous appraisals indicated. I am just not going to think about it."

"You're right, but it'll be difficult not to," Shirley stated.

"What time is it?"

"Fifteen minutes after two."

"I have to go now. I wanted to report to work much earlier. I'll have to talk with you later. Bye."

"Don't you want to kiss me?" Shirley asked.

"Oh, I'm sorry. Sure." We kissed. "I have to go. Bye."

As I got into my car, one of my neighbors, Cathy, stopped me briefly and asked, "Where are you going all dressed up in your suit and overcoat?"

I said, "I'm going to work."

"Midday?"

"Yes. I am reporting to work for the second shift operations."

"New job?" she asked.

"No, it's not a new job. I'm going back to work at General Motors. They called me last Thursday evening informing me I was required to report today. I reported to work this morning, but after holding several discussions regarding my return, they finally decided to put me on second shift."

"Second shift? How dreadful."

"I know what you must think, Cathy, about working on second shift. At this particular plant General Motors runs three shifts. There was some talk that they were thinking of putting me on third shift to run the manufacturing operations, as I will be required on second shift. It could have been worse, since I would be one of the only management workers on third shift with several workers under me. Don't get me wrong. It doesn't really matter to me what shift I work, because I am going to do the best job I can. I know if Denis, who is in charge of one area of the manufacturing operations, were to have his way he would put me on third shift, as he told me earlier. He told me, 'I want to put you on third shift to run manufacturing activity there alone. You'd be out of the way of the others.' I don't know what he meant by this. I thought he would only be concerned about my talents and contributions to General Motors.

"Besides, Cathy, I have to work to support my family. I don't have a choice. These people seem to be playing with my life and there is nothing I can do about it. I have no other choice but to do as they tell me and do it exceptionally well. I'm in a glass house filled with crystal."

"What do you mean?" Cathy asked.

"Well, it's like this . . . ." I started to explain, but didn't want to risk being late for work, so I excused myself and left.

As I approached the General Motors facility in Oak Creek, Wisconsin, I was greeted by several UA workers who pleasantly greeted me and welcomed my return. I noticed that Ralph and Mary, two individuals of the group who had previously worked for me, wanted to talk to me. I waved to them both and stated, "I would love to chat but I am running slightly behind schedule. I have to go into the plant now."

I opened the doors to the facility of the GM offices and was greeted by the Sergeant of Security, Larry. He asked for my identification. I told him I had turned it in to Gil and Joe in the financial group when I left in December and no one had given me a new security identification card upon my return. He said, "Well, Gary, you'll have to sign in and wait until I can clear you through Personnel."

I knew I'd have to sign in, but I didn't think I'd have to wait in the lobby since all visitors are allowed to sign in and immediately go to the waiting area. "You are asking that I wait at the door for further instruction, correct?"

"Yes," he stated.

I said, "Fine. It's okay with me."

As I stood at the door, several workers, management and Union, passed and greeted me. I nodded my head slightly to greet them but refrained from going into any detail about my controversial return to the company. I did not say anything at all.

I looked at the clock on the wall of the facility. It still had 30 minutes before the shift began. Larry turned toward me as he hung up the phone and said the people I was scheduled to meet were not in their offices.

I said, "Then where are they?"

He said, "I checked upstairs with their secretaries and no one knows where they are."

"Is it possible for you to call upstairs and have them paged?" I asked.

"Well, I don't know if I should do that."

"Are you saying I can go upstairs now?"

"I'm not saying you can go upstairs, either."

"Then I would appreciate it if you could have them paged. I would like to meet with them to discuss my assignment this evening."

The sergeant made a phone call, but I did not know with whom he was talking. I wanted him to resolve this without my having to go over his head. Shortly, two other security guards reported to the security station at the plant entrance. They had a brief discussion among themselves. I interrupted the sergeant and said, "Have you heard from Personnel yet?"

The sergeant replied, "No."

"I would like you to call them now. I have to meet with them before the shift begins. I am trying to cooperate with you regarding plant security procedures, however, I need to be upstairs now. If you cannot page them, you can walk with me upstairs to Personnel."

"That won't be necessary. Let me try having them paged as you suggested," the sergeant said.

Five minutes went by before Tom from Personnel authorized my entry to the administrative offices.

Tom and Bonnie asked that I come into a room next to the waiting area. They asked if I had given any thought to signing the release.

"Bonnie and I went through this extensively this morning and my position now is the same as it was then. I will not sign a release of any kind. Are you asking me to report back to work or not?" I asked.

Tom and Bonnie both had uncomfortable expressions and disappointment on their faces. Tom without hesitation stated, "You are required to report to Dave and you will be working for him on second shift. You have five minutes to report to him before the shift begins."

"He's located in the first office on Mahogany Row," Bonnie said.

I said, "Okay. Do you have any additional comments?"

Bonnie said, "If I were you, I would think about signing that . . . ."

"I have to go now to report to work. I am certain I will see you again in the near future."

Dave's office was filled with smoke from cigarettes and cigars from those who were in the office shortly before I got there. I found Dave behind his desk, which was filled with several documents, most notably production schedules and material reports.

He lifted his head as I entered his office and said, "I understand you'll be working for me in Sections One and Two of the plant."

"No one told me specifically which section I would work in. They only told me to report to you."

"I decided to work you in Sections One and Two of manufacturing operations. I know you spent all of your time in Section Three and Building Three of our manufacturing operations, but you'll be required to manage and work on all lines in Sections One and Two. I expect production requirements to be met on all lines as assigned."

"This won't be a problem for me. You know I always meet my production and management goals with the highest standard of quality. I have consistently demonstrated outstanding results with my responsibilities. Quite simply, Dave, you will not have any problems with my performance."

"Well, I was told you have lost your effectiveness as an outstanding manager because of the way you were treated by that group in the financial area," Dave said.

"My treatment in the financial area is still a mystery to me, Dave. I do not know why the financial people did not focus on developing me in order for me to continue my move up the corporate ladder. Now it has been jeopardized by those who did not want me to succeed. I don't know why I was treated that way, and I prefer not to have any future discussions with anyone regarding my involvement with the financial people. Right now, the only thing I want to do is focus on putting my career back together.

"I know I am considered an adversary by the company and several of my co-workers. The only thing I want to do is regain the respect I had before in the financial area of the company. I hope you can be objective, Dave. I know you, of all people, are completely a company man, a team player, and that it may be difficult for you to properly and fairly reflect my performance in manufacturing, given the fact that the company is at odds with me."

"Well, Gary, I can't say I know what really happened to you and your career in the financial organization, but I will pay close attention to your performance in manufacturing."

"I know, Dave, however, the job I do will be done under close watch simply because I am now considered an adversary; I still have unresolved issues pending with the company. I don't think you will have much input as to my actual performance; any such input will be developed by others."

"No one will interfere in how I rate your performance."

"Dave, listen to me. I just want you to know that I have a feeling my performance rating will be tempered by management and others as a result of my involvement with the company and what happened to me in the financial group. I just want you to know I'm not stupid or naive when it comes to the company's motives and their decision to bring me back. There is a reason for doing this, and I am certain it's for their benefit.

"Now that I've gotten that off my chest, Dave, let's go to work."

"Gary, I am certain that what happened to you in the financial group . . . ."

"Dave, I'm done with that. Let's go forward. I do not want to discuss what happened to me with you or anyone during my assignment to manufacturing. Do you understand?"

"Yes, I understand, however . . . ."

"Dave, come on. Let's get to work. Where is my assignment?"

Dave shook his head and said, "We are assigning you to manage the operations on Lines One and Two and Sections One and Two. I am aware that you have worked in Section Three and Building Three and have had some exposure to the pressroom. We decided to put you in Sections One and Two to give you additional exposure to our plant operations. You'll find it is much different from the other areas of the plant where you worked."

"Yes, I know. We have different equipment, and the manufacturing requirements and intricacies are different in each section of the plant. Remember, I used to work here? Forget what rumors you may have heard regarding my situation and think back when I used to work almost side by side with you in Section Three before my assignment to the financial group."

"Yeah, I know that, Gary, but that was some time ago. In fact, several years ago if I'm not mistaken."

"It was about two years ago, Dave. I've not been gone that long, and keep in mind, I was looking at the company from a different perspective. Now, just show me my people."

"What about running the electron beam welding process, Gary? Are you familiar with it?"

"Well, according to a manual about the operations I once read, it consists of A, B and C rooms on Line Two. It has lead chambers to protect operators from radiation exposure, and its critical points are the mechanical interface of X, Y and Z axis and the electrical circuitry of the electron beam unit itself, which is governed by the external interface of two separate computers that deliver commands to the modicum of the operation itself. Operators of the process are required to wear radiation badges and utilize radiation detection equipment to determine any exposure or leakage of radiation."

"Damn it. Stop, Gary. You don't need to go to any great extent telling me everything there is about the operation."

"Well, you asked. Now, Dave, since you have interrupted me, just show me my people so I can begin to run my area of responsibility."

"Gary, slow down. I'll let you know who your people are later. But first, do you have any questions about anything?"

"Well, if all the line operation specification manuals and product blueprints are in order and in the proper place, and I have the required amount of personnel to run my operations effectively, I'll say no, I don't have any additional questions."

"Then I will show you your people."

On our way to the location of my people, several managers greeted me as Dave and I continued our tour.

Dave and I approached the group of people who would be working for me, in the area of the plant where workers take their coffee breaks. There are several of these break areas throughout the plant. Occasionally members of management would gather at these locations to hold "shop talk," daily conversations about the operations. Several internal arrangements came out of these mini-meetings and a closeness developed. Workers and managers both got a lot more done by participating in these daily discussions. Sometimes one could get several additional benefits from participating, aside from just the social nature of it. One could get additional people and in-process materials to keep his operations running when there were shortages of materials or labor. These shop talk conversations also provided information regarding the company itself. A lot of the information was without substantiation, but some was factual.

Most of the people who were assigned to me were in the satellite area having coffee and other refreshments. Dave yelled to the crew, "Listen up, people. Can I have your attention for a moment? Gary here will be your manager. You will be working for him directly. That's all I have to say. Do you have anything to say, Gary?"

"Yes. May I have everyone's attention? I see some new faces in the area. For those of you who are not familiar with me, let me introduce myself. My name is

Gary McKnight and I will be responsible for the operation in Sections One and Two, Line Two, however, occasionally it will be required that you work on other lines and sections of the plant. I will need your cooperation in this regard. Also, I will need you to give me your best efforts on a daily basis. We need to maintain our competitiveness and build a high-quality product. This will mean more for everyone eventually. If you do the things you are required to do as planned, you will not have any problems from me at all. If things do not go as planned and you don't at least try to give me your best efforts, then and only then will we have problems. I am certain we will do just fine and you will not disappoint me.

"The shift begins at 3:00 p.m. and ends at 11:30 p.m. Now, I know you are working as extras throughout the plant, so I am not going to hold you any longer. I look forward to having all of you join my team. You can safely go back to your work areas now. Thank you for your attention."

"Gary, listen to me. I asked if you had anything to say, not if you'd give them a lecture," Dave said.

"Dave, look, I know my returning to work under these circumstances has placed me at odds with the company and several individuals. However, I expect to do the best job I possibly can for the company since I know anything I do from here on out will be carefully watched and possibly held against me. Therefore, since I cannot tell the people who work for me anything at all about my situation with the company, I have to make certain they understand fully what I expect of them. Now what I need is your cooperation as well, in order for me to do my job effectively. I also need to know is if you'll be fair and objective regarding my performance, or if you'll be a team player for the company and participate in their efforts to discredit me because of my administrative charges against them? Can you be fair, Dave?"

"Gary, I think I am fair, and you ought not be concerned about your problem between you and the company. I know nothing about that."

"Dave, several people around here know about my situation with the company. How they know about it is anyone's guess. What I do know is that I have not mentioned it to anyone. But Dave, let's get on with running this business and running it exceptionally well and not make my involvement an issue here.

"You, of all people, know there are many different management styles and the approach I've just taken with a crew of people, who are working for five different managers with different management styles, is what I needed to get their attention. Now, Dave, let's move on. I have work to do and I don't want my involvement with the company to cause a problem. Certainly under normal circumstances, if I were not involved in an unfavorable bout with the company, I could be more direct with my people, an approach you could get away with regardless of what complaints are lodged against you by one of your Union employees. Even if the United Auto Workers Union committee representative was to file a grievance against you because of your approach or unfair labor practice, the complaint would not end up in your appraisal as an unfavorable rating. However, I am certain it would end up in mine without a second thought. Now, Dave, let's move on. Show me the routings for the plenum assembly operations. I understand several changes have been made."

"Yes, several changes have been made and it is in the front of Line One, Section One of Building Two. Before we get to that, Gary, I want to . . . . Wait, Gary. I am being paged, hold on. Yeah, this is Dave. What happened? Bob, you've got to be kidding. How long have you been down? Two hours? Where are you now? I'll be over to help. You get that equipment up and running. How long have you had someone working on it? What? I'll be right there. Look, I have to run over to Line Six EBs. Bob's having equipment problems."

"What's the problem Dave?"

"He had a tooling crash and may have had some tears in the rooms. I don't know. God damn, those damn parts are hot and there's no surge ahead of Section Three. We have to get that damn line running."

"If you don't need me on Line Six, since you and Bob are over there, I would like to look at those routings for the preassemble operation we talked about in Section One."

"I can't help you with that."

"Dave, I know. Why don't you go to Line Six to help Bob? I'm already familiar with the operations. I just want to review the routings for new changes."

I was glad Dave had to go help Bob with his production problems because it appeared Dave did not accept my views regarding the management approach I had taken. Dave seemed to be making an issue of the conversation with the group of people who were scheduled to work for me the next day. Somehow, he knew he had to get me to manage the people as he and several other managers did, with a firm approach. However, I was certain Dave knew it was too soon and not appropriate for me to be as firm with my people as he is with his. I wanted my workers to understand my management style; and besides, I had a different objective. Dave did not necessarily care for my viewpoint, or whether or not I alienated my group of people.

For me to have employee grievance problems would give General Motors the fuel they needed to fire me on the spot, although General Motors could fire a member of management any time it wanted to. However, it was important for them to carefully structure my termination with the giant automotive company, since my previous performance in this area had been highly effective to outstanding. I now expected the company to begin readjusting my performance ratings in order to justify getting rid of me. Although it was my first day back, it appeared as if Dave wanted to start something with me that he could use against me later. It would allow him to give me a low rating, which would affect my ability to advance and hinder future wage increases. From this day on I knew without question it would be a very difficult relationship. I was considered an outcast for protecting my employment rights.

I saw it as a catch 22 situation. If I did nothing about the violations at all, they would occur again and affect someone else. If I chose to continue to pursue the issues before the Labor Department, General Motors would inevitably continue its efforts to infringe upon my reputation as a good manager for the company. At this point I was considered an outcast because I had no other choice but to bring charges against the giant corporation.

I knew from the very beginning the company had developed a plan to get rid of me. However, I knew I had to do everything correctly. There were no allowances for error. For one thing, my relationship with the company was not good. It was almost as if I were one of the competitors, a Lee Iaccoca, or for that matter, Ralph Nader or Warren Beaver.

Although I knew I could have used a more aggressive and direct management approach with my people, as Dave had indicated, I rejected that style for the moment because I knew the company was not on my side at all. I needed to build my own organization within the company. The approach Dave recommended was okay for him because he was not at odds with the company. This more direct approach would have caused me substantial problems and would be evidenced by formal complaints filed against me by the Union. This would mean that not only would I be tussling with General Motors, but I'd also be at odds with the United Auto Workers Union. However, I knew eventually I would have to use various management approaches in order to get the results I needed, and at times this would also include the direct methods.

Moments later, Dave suddenly appeared in my sight again as he walked through a manual entrance cut in the conveyor section of one of the highly automated lines of Line Three, Section Two. Dave's appearance indicated he was extremely upset about the production problems on Line Six. He was flustered; his face had turned from white to beet red, and clouds of smoke surfaced above his head. His eyes were protruding as if they were inflated. He was about to explode with anger at any moment, and he was heading in my direction. He stopped at the desk on Line Three between Sections One and Two in the plant.

He snatched up the black phone and slammed it down on the desk, causing several items to move. He lifted the receiver and began yelling into the phone. In the middle of his conversation, he lifted his portable pager to his other ear, talking on the phone at the same time. Throughout the entire time he had a cloud of smoke surrounding his head. He seemed to be inhaling deeply. As soon as he placed the receiver down on the base of the black phone, he snatched it up again. When he completed dialing, his portable pager went off again. He began talking into the receiver, his face getting bright red and his eyes and the veins in his neck swelling. He shook his head, looked up at the ceiling, and turned in a small circle while reaching for the broken pack of cigarettes on the desk. He once more slammed the phone on the desk and as he lifted some papers from the desk, shoving them under his arm, he began to briskly walk in my direction. He suddenly stopped and lit a cigarette, then resumed walking briskly in my direction.

I did not know exactly what occurred, other than the equipment problems on Line Six with Bob. However, I could see he was not in a good mood. He continued his brisk walk in my direction, smoking his cigarette and tightly holding several papers under his arm. He quickened his walking pace. His angry appearance did not change from his travel from Line Six, Section One to the pressroom entrance. At that point, he lit another cigarette.

I once again shouted out to him, above the noise coming from the heavy machinery of the plant, "Can I help you, Dave?"

He stopped momentarily as if he heard something but quickly began walking into the pressroom and was soon beyond sight. He never turned to reply. As I looked in his direction, I saw a cloud of smoke hovering above his head before he suddenly disappeared between the two large presses.

The evening passed rather quickly. Fifteen minutes remained in the shift. In the short amount of time left, I completed my review of the routing changes of the line operations for which I was responsible. On my way out of the plant at 11:45 p.m., I walked past the disabled 1800 ton press. Dave was standing with two other managers and two skilled tradesmen who were pulling the die block out of the press housing with a hoist. Dave was talking with the two managers responsible for the 1800 ton presses. He paced back and forth in a short, narrow path with one hand on his hip near his pager and a cigarette in the other.

Somehow Dave managed to contain his anger about operational problems that night. He did not blow up with the managers, outwardly. Looking at him you could see his balls were in a vice and he was about ready to explode regarding the equipment problems.

As I continued my travels, one of the managers and skilled tradesmen called out, "Good night."

I responded, "Good night." On my way out of the plant I thought to myself my first day back could have been a complete disaster.

CHAPTER III

Industrial Espionage

On a clear night, as the moon appeared brightly lit, I began driving home and briefly reflected upon the events that occurred in the plant. I knew from this moment I would have a difficult time with the corporation and management. My career was over.

Although someone else's management style, the way they managed me and handled my employment issues, would be the primary reason to file charges with the Department of Labor and Industry, I knew after I had filed the charge there was nothing else I could do other than live with my decision and begin a process of negotiation with the world's largest corporation.

Quite simply, I felt what happened to me was wrongful and preventable. Although I worked endlessly and extensively for the company, my decision to file charges against management and challenge their decision not to follow procedure forced me to accept that my career would forever be forsaken with the giant organization. The dream I had as a young man to work for General Motors was gone forever. I suddenly realized I would have to accept this fact early on, stay focused on all my responsibilities and continue to do the best job I possibly could for the company, regardless of the outcome.

This thought was confirmed when I thought about how Dave discussed the requirements of my assignment upon my return. This was direct evidence my relationship with the giant automotive company had changed for the worst. The relationship, which was once a good one, was beginning to crumble and I was now an outcast, another of General Motors' adversaries. Not only would I have the responsibility of managing people and facilities of this industrial company, I would also be required to contend with everything else that came out of this legal involvement.

Everything I did and said would be carefully monitored and documented and later used against me in my appraisal or a court of law, if necessary. It was my intent to do whatever was professionally necessary to completely resolve this strife with the giant industrialist.

"Gary, is that you?" my wife asked.

"Yes," I said.

"How did things go?"

"Okay. Things were okay."

"Are you sure? You don't sound if things were okay."

"Well, you know. Things aren't going to be the way they once were. I don't think company officials are too pleased with me now that I've filed charges against them with the Department of Labor. But there was nothing else I could do."

"Well, maybe you should have left the company."

"Maybe. Maybe not. As you can gather, I chose not to leave. I am not the kind of person to just simply give up and allow someone to conduct a deliberate wrong against me. Just because these people do not understand me or like me for whatever reason, that does not give them the right to treat me, or anyone for that matter, adversely. And besides, if I just left, walked away from it all, what would that accomplish? Absolutely nothing because they would just do it to someone else who may not be able to stand up for himself."

"Honey, why do you have to be the one to challenge General Motors?"

"Why? Because this is my career and my dream these people are fucking with! Don't you understand? They are fucking with my life, my dreams and our family! We have kids, you know; kids I'm responsible for raising! And besides, who fucking else is going to stand up for his rights against General Motors?

"I somehow was mysteriously injured on the job following several hostile confrontations initiated by my immediate manager, and I need to find out what happened. Why did it happen? It could have been avoided. I did everything I could to get from underneath this guy. What happened to me did not have to happen. Besides, if I don't get this matter resolved within the corporation through the open door policy with the Department of Labor and Industry, I'll have to go through the courts. If I have to litigate this goddamned thing, then, goddamn it, I will. Who do they think they are fucking with anyway?"

"Gary, what are you doing? Why are you swearing? You don't swear."

"I know. I'm sorry. I'm sorry if this is upsetting you. I know this is not me. I generally don't react like this. When I get into a fight with someone, I am in it and it's over with. I don't have to do a lot of swearing. However, this is a different kind of fight. I just don't like someone setting me up like they did at General Motors. They actually set me up to fail. After my assignment to the financial area of General Motors, in spite of my extensive effort, work responsibility and contribution. I don't understand this. There is no reason for the way I was treated, no reason whatsoever. This is my career, my life, our life, they are interfering with. If I do nothing, it will be someone else's. Don't you understand? You saw what happened to me. You knew what I went through. Now, I have to do the best I can. I do not have the support of the company. You know that, don't you?"

"Yes, Gary, I know how you were treated."

"Shirley, you know we have a busy schedule ahead of us tomorrow. Let's go to bed."

"Yeah, you're right. Lets go to bed."

*   *   *

"Okay, listen here. Now that I have you to myself and you know me and what I expect, from all who were present during my introduction yesterday in the satellite area, we will be running Line One, Sections One and Two through final EBs. Now remember, each and every one of us has a responsibility to our customers, the company and ourselves if we want to be competitive and remain the major player in this automotive market. We want to stay focused on our customers' needs and the quality of our product.

"As you know, we must build it right the first time, and the rest will follow. Now, let's go get 'em.

"Hey, Gary."

"Yeah," I said, as I heard someone call my name from a distance above the noise level of the machines."

"Hi Gary."

"Hi, Kathy. Hi Margaret."

"It's good to see you," Margaret said.

"Yeah, right. I'm glad to see you also."

"How does it feel to be back?" asked Kathy.

"It seems as if I never left. It's good to be back. Where are you two going?"

"Up front to a management meeting in the conference room. Aren't you going?"

"No, I'm not going. I didn't get information on that one."

"Ah, come on. You must have."

"No, I didn't see anything in my box. Listen, go ahead to the meeting without me. After all I have to be certain everything goes right. I have a lot of new workers in my area and I want to make sure I'm around for them if they have questions. Thanks for letting me know about the meeting."

"Okay, we'll see you later Gary."

Then from another direction I heard, "Mr. McKnight, Mr. McKnight."

"Yes, Gail? Oh, by the way, call me Gary. How can I help you?"

"We're running out of material for the line."

"What do you need exactly?"

"Everything."

"No problem. Done. Sam? I need a complete line set-up of parts from the pressroom."

"Okay, I'll get it when I come back from Line Six. By the way, the pressroom is running low on parts, too."

"Well, it's important I get this material now. I'm about to run out of parts. You don't' want to bump my line by causing me to run out of parts, because then I would not be in a good mood. I need the parts now. See what you can do. Thanks. Start by bringing me two baskets of upper and lower shell halves and two baskets of upper and lower retainers."

"Here's your two baskets of upper and lower shell halves, and I put the retainers on the from end of the line", Sam said when he returned.

"Thanks, Sam. I knew you could do it."

"Next time Gary, you'll have to get the driver assigned to your area."

"Yeah, I know Sam. Either he's not assigned or he has not shown up. Let me put in a page from his boss. In the mean time, I need you to feed the welders before the second half of the line goes down . . . and keep the line full with parts until my driver gets here. Thanks."

"Okay."

The General Motors plant operations which housed its manufacturing lines was an elaborate maze of various machinery and equipment. The industrial environment was a carefully arranged system of manufacturing resources so its workers could complete their assignments in a safe and effective manner. Most often everyone was so involved in his work he did not hear the thundering sounds of the machinery and equipment, and occasionally many of the workers forgot their hearing equipment. It requires supervision to enforce the requirement of workers protection.

Every day from now on would be a new day at General Motors, having to prove myself beyond that of others, with no room for mistakes of any kind. I had to carefully develop a strategy to deliver the most effective results. I new the would scrutinize everything I did wrong and not take into consideration anything I did right. They began to document everything I did to use it against me sometime I the future. Eventually, it most likely would result in termination of my employment. However, I remained focused on completing all my assignments to the fullest extent. It was difficult for most of my people, as I was required to manage them closely. Other member of management were concerned for their position and didn't support my work efforts.

Inevitably this matter had to be litigated in court for resolution. The company did not seem intimidated by the Labor Department. However, I would not allow the company or anyone to intimidate me either. I just had to manage my own. My decision to file the charge with the Department of Labor and Industry was final, that is, at least until General Motors official decided to resolved our differenced. Before this ordeal was over, General Motors involved other in their effort to facilitate my termination. I did not quite understand why the Department of

Labor and Industry did not require General Motors to transfer me out of this particular location. More abuse followed as a result of the complaint I filed with the Labor Department?

* * *

"Gary?"

"Yeah, Dave? What do you need?"

"How did you do last night?" Dave asked.

"Just fine. We exceeded our requirement by 200 units and each unit was high quality. Didn't you see the production report?"

"Yeah, I saw it. I mean how were the people? Did you have any problems with your people?"

"No. they did a good job. The schedule called for 2,750 units, we completed 2,950. they did just fine. The line needs to be fine-tuned to continue giving us good results, but it's nothing you need to be concerned about. I'll take care of it myself. Speaking of line, I need you to run regular requirements on line."

"What is it now? Hold on. Let me answer this page."

"Dave, wait. What were you going to say?"

"Not now, Gary! Hold on! I have to get my page!"

Dave walked to the middle of Line Two and picked up the phone. He seemed angry. He quickly put out one cigarette and lit another one. Before hi finished his conversation he put that one out and lit another one. He gripped his cigarette and a cup of coffee with one hand and the telephone with the other. It appeared as if he had concerns elsewhere. Soon he disappeared from the line.

As I went to the other side of the line, I saw him once again going into the pressroom where GM houses its gigantic 1800 ton presses. This was where the units for my section's production were made. The units I built traveled from Sections One and Two for final assembly in Section Three.

Obviously Dave wanted to run something other than Line One. He was looking at Line Three, and Line Two was in preventative maintenance. Line Three was not set up with in-process inventory, but Line One was fully set up for production. Obviously, Line Three was a hot line and those requirements were needed. I checked the schedule which showed Line One for production. I looked at what the first shift manager ran, and the intershift. According to the intershift, the nucor, (for shell assembly) machine was down for three hours and a helluva lot of production time had been lost due to a pneumatic cylinder and a broken shaft on the transfer of that machine. Line One looked good with plenty of inventory ahead of Sections Two and Three.

Where the hell was Dave? I was already two minutes into my shift and was getting impatient. I was scheduled for Line One tonight. I checked to see what

Line Three had in front of Section Three—nothing. Section Three would not run tonight if there was nothing here. I paged Dave to get the okay to run Line Three because I didn't want any problems. I couldn't make any mistakes whatsoever.

"Dave, call line one, McKnight," I paged, but there was no answer.

My crew was ready to go. I had to call this one. "Okay, people, listen up. We will be running Line Three this evening until further notice."

After one hour into the shift, Dave appeared. "Gary, Gary," he yelled as he entered Building Two from the pressroom. "How did you know I wanted to run Line Three tonight?"

"Well, you did, didn't you?"

"Well, not really. I didn't have any choice. First shift missed their schedule and shipping is waiting for everything we can run, straight back. Goddamn it. I don't fucking believe it . . . all fucking day on that goddamned nucor machine. Can you believe it?"

"Well, I guess we'll just have to complete the schedule. Everything's going fine now."

"Why didn't you page me?"

"I did page you, Dave. You didn't return my call."

"I didn't hear the page. This fucking thing went off once since the beginning of the shift. My fucking batteries must be low."

"Yeah, must be. Well, do you want me to continue running on this line?"

"I thought I could get another crew, but we're short people throughout the plant."

"I can take my people off the line now and send them back to their regular line."

"No, that won't be necessary. We need the parts on Line Three."

"Well, okay. Line One is now in good shape as far as having sufficient in-process inventory to keep the line shift going from front to back. Operationally things are just fine there."

"Good. Let's see if we can keep Line Three on schedule."

"Okay, job's done."

Several months passed and on many occasions I was confronted with the same line condition. I would have to continually reassign my people, after talking with Dave, in order to complete the schedule of a previous line shift operation.

No line is completely trouble free, however, it is up to the manager to balance his or her resources to minimize the down time of the line. On every occasion my team continued to meet the schedule of our line shift with the highest possible quality for each part for our customers.

Throughout the next several months there were no complaints alleged against me. Each time I completed my schedule Dave would say, "Good job, Gary."

The pager sounded. Beep . . . beep . . . beep . . . beep.

"Damn it," said Dave. "What now? I've got to answer this goddamned page. I've been having problems on Line Six and in the pressroom."

Well, it was better that he was having problems everywhere else except my line. I didn't need any problems, but I was sure they would come.

"Hey, Gary," said a voice.

"Yeah? Hey, Wilbert, how the hell are . . . ."

"Okay. How the fuck are you man? God damn, don't you come up for air sometimes?"

"No, man, I can't. You know my situation, Wilbert. I am an adversary. General Motors is documenting every fucking thing I do. I can't stop to breathe. I have to be on top of everything. You know that."

"Yeah, I know. In fact, I was told to stay away from you myself."

"Oh, yeah?"

Wilbert nodded yes.

"Who told you that?"

"My boss, Bill."

"You've got to be kidding."

"No, man. I wouldn't kid you. Not me."

"What did he say exactly, and when?"

"He said it when you first got back, and he has said several times since then."

"How did he say it, Wilbert?"

"He said, `Listen, stay away from McKnight. He is a political hot potato and if you value your career you'll stay away from him.' He said it to the entire group of managers."

"Did he tell you why?"

"Yeah. He said you filed a lawsuit against the company and that's why they brought you back. Several people were not too pleased that you're suing the company."

"Wilbert, I had no choice, other than to file charges with the Department of Labor and Industry. I was selected for layoff inappropriately with no regard for my seniority. The open door to discuss problems of this kind with upper management was closed. I had no other choice. I had to file. My performance was previously rated highly effective to outstanding. How do you explain how I was treated in the financial area of the business? Quite simply, that treatment was uncalled for. I was working for the best interest of this god damned company and somehow I was mysteriously injured, subsequently laid off out of seniority and had several other entitlements taken away. What else was I supposed to do? I had no choice. I had to do it. But you know what the strangest thing is about this situation?"

"What?" asked Wilbert.

"I was on my way to the top, and I was told to stay away from you. I didn't because everything I did I did very well, as my appraisal indicated. I did not have to concern myself with staying away from you. Now the table has turned. They want you to stay away from me because of someone else, namely the folks upstairs in the financial organization. But no matter who started it, I have to finish it. It's my career, my fucking career. Excuse the French, Wilbert."

"No, go ahead. I understand, Gary, man. I would be fucking upset, too, if it were mine."

"Well, Wilbert, you know no matter what I do or how well I do it my career is over and eventually they are going to terminate me anyway."

"Well, I'm no longer a team player in their eyes. You know that, don't you?"

"Yeah, I guess you're probably right. Neither am I, for that matter. You didn't have to sue them or bring charges before the Department of Labor so you're okay, Wilbert. You're okay. I have to go. My people are coming back from lunch. We'll talk some other time. Thanks for the tip."

"Yeah. No problem. Anytime."

"Wayne, Ricky, give me your counts. Thanks. Excellent. Let's do it again tomorrow, people. Good night."

"Good night, Gary."

"Good night ladies. I'll see you tomorrow."

"Gary . . . Gary?"

"Who the hell is calling me now?" It sounded like Bonnie, and it was Bonnie. "What do you want?"

"We need to talk, Gary."

"Talk? What about?"

"You know. Don't kid me now."

"No, I don't know. Be specific."

"You have some unfinished business to take care of."

"What's that?"

"This release."

"Release? What release?"

"The release you forgot to . . . well, the release you didn't sign before."

"Oh, that release. Well, I told you before I was not going to sign it until the company resolves my concerns as set forth in the complaint with the Labor Department."

"Well, the Labor Department said you had to sign it as a condition for getting your job back."

"I did not agree to that. I want all my issues in that complaint to be addressed."

"Well, you're going to have to sign it."

"I am telling you I am not going to sign anything! Do you hear me?! Now, get out of my face with this! I have a job to do!"

"Hey, Boss, McKnight?"

"Yeah?"

"Where are we running tonight?"

"We're running specials on Line Four. Set up and let's go get 'em."

Poump! Poump! Poump! Poump! Soon the thundering sounds of the machines began and continued until the first break, then for the balance of the shift.

"Helen, put on your hearing protection. Thank you. Richard, start the conveyor on your exit machine. Thank you. Let's go, now. Let's move. Let's put it all together, people."

Several months passed. We continued to run production in my area without any significant incidents or production problems. It was a job well done.

My method of managing the people in my particular work group became more focused on doing the best job I could and working closely with my people as well, since the corporation was still at odds with me. I knew as soon as General Motors determined the strengths and weaknesses of the issues of my charges against them and the effectiveness of my attorney, as well as the system which handled it, it would eventually make quick decisions regarding my existence as a manager. Soon I would be reassigned to work for others who would play a significant role in whatever happened to me at GM.

I ventured a guess that eventually General Motors would terminate me, although this was not a remote possibility. However, this was not exactly what I wanted. That's why my commitment to work was unrelenting, as I would put my best efforts to managing people and resources as intelligently as possible. This job was important to me, especially since I was more than one thousand miles from where I was accustomed to being.

"Gary, listen up," said Dave. "After you get your area going, Pat Thompson would like to see you up front on Mahogany Row."

"What for?"

"I guess according to directives from upstairs she's coming to manufacturing and, uh, you're assigned to work with her."

"With her or for her, Dave?"

"You know what I mean, Gary!"

"Yeah, I guess I do."

"Let me get this going and then I'll go up front, Dave."

Beep . . . beep . . . beep . . . beep . . . beep . . . beep.

"Hold on, Gary. Someone is trying to contact me."

Dave quickly walked across to Line Two to use the phone. Shortly afterwards, he was talking firmly into the phone and quickly inhaling and exhaling cigarette smoke. Then, he slammed the receiver of the phone on its base with great precision and began walking in my direction.

"Dave, I will talk . . . ."

"Not now, Gary. I've got a damned press down in the fucking pressroom. I've got to go . . . ."

"Yeah. See ya . . . ."

"Hey, Gary?" It was Pat. "Did you see Dave? Where did he go?"

"He should be in the pressroom."

"Did he tell you yet?"

"Tell me what?"

"That you are going to be working with me now."

"Yeah, he did mention something like that."

"I see your area is running very well."

"Yeah, you could say that. Generally, it runs that way all the time."

"I can see you have several difficult employees working for you."

"No, Pat, not really. I have a good team here, and as long as they produce for me that's really all that matters."

"Well, that's more than what I'd say about them."

"Listen, Pat. I know the company is getting you involved in my particular matter with them. I guess there's more to your being brought downstairs to work with me. You're part of GM's strategy of a well orchestrated termination. I guess there's no stopping this is there?"

"Stopping what, Gary?"

"Pat, why don't you just stop? You know what I'm talking about. The company wants to fire me. There's just no stopping it, and you know it. Regardless of what I do, General Motors is going to terminate me simply because I brought charges against them before the Department of Labor and Industry and because I refused to sign the release with the company officials, dropping the complaint. My attorney . . . ."

"Well, Gary, I don't see what this has to do with us."

"Pat, eventually General Motors is going to simply use you as another witness against me to prove their case. No matter what I do, the company is going to terminate me. I saw it with Dave."

"That's not true, Gary. I'll take care of you. I'm not here to terminate you."

"Listen, Pat. Off the record, there was a time I was highly regarded, considered one of the company's best managers with a lot of promise to move to the very top of this company. Now look at the situation I'm in. I can't even sit still. I can't sit down for even a fucking minute because everything has to go perfectly or I will be held responsible for it."

"No, Gary. Listen to me. You're wrong . . . dead wrong. You give me what I want and I'll take care of you. Give me everything you've got and you won't have any problems at all."

"Pat, time out. Listen to me. You cannot stop what's going to happen here. General Motors wants my fucking balls and you know. Everyone knows. My employees know it; you can't stop it."

"You're wrong, Gary."

"Watch. Keep your eyes and ears open, Pat. I'm not going to think about this. I don't talk to the employees about it. No one here knows my views about this at all. This conversation between you and me is to let you know I know what's going on. I go out of my way to do more work than is required. You know that, don't you?"

"I'll see, Gary, although you have been known to do a very good job in this area."

"Well, Pat, let's say I still do. I get good results. I make certain of that. Let's talk tomorrow, okay? You have other people you may want to talk with and I don't want my people to get restless. I have to stay on top of things, you know."

Several months passed. Although my production and quality requirements were without incident, I imagined soon there would be some adverse developments.

"Gary?" said Pat. "I want to talk with you when you get your area running."

"Sure. I'll be with you shortly," I said, then I went to make certain things were going without incident.

"Yeah, Pat? What did you want to talk about?"

"Well, I was talking with Bob and understand he was short of people last night. He said you were very difficult with him and told him to get out of your area and leave you alone, that you could not help him. Is that what you said, Gary? Answer me! Is that what you said?"

"Pat, listen to me. First of all, I can't believe we're having this conversation. You know the staffing in my department is so fucking tight it's unbelievable that I meet my production requirements all the time. Of course, my people are also concerned about this because they do not have as much help as the other departments. You know I'm running short because we talked about it before. So does Bob. I can't believe this. It's the company, right? Pat, tell me. This is what General Motors wants you to document, isn't it? More dissension between me and my peers."

"No, Gary, that's not it at all."

"To answer your question about what I told Bob, quite simply I told him I was short on people and that he should contact you and other departments that have extra people. By design, my department does not have the extra people it needs, or for that matter any extra people period, not even for my needs. I hope you understand what I am saying."

"No, Gary, I don't. You have to have someone I can take off your line."

"Pat, I don't have any extra people. The staffing of people in my department is very tight. You ought to know that by now. I would not try to deceive you at all. I am running without a trucker now, and that simply upsets the hell out of my people. They're complaining now."

Beep . . . beep . . . . beep . . . . beep . . . beep. The pager attached to her waist went off.

"Goddamn it What the . . . ?"

Beep . . . beep . . . beep. "Pat, call 3636, pressroom, Bart."

"Damn it. What now? I've been over there most of the shift," replied Pat. "Don't tell me his press is down."

"Well, if it is, Pat, you could give Bob those extra people he's been looking for while your operations are idle."

"God damn it, Gary. Don't play games with me now. I'm not in a good mood."

"I'm only trying to make a suggestion, Pat. You said you needed people for Bob, now go get them."

"Damn it! I certainly didn't need them this way. I've been catching hell about that damned pressroom. Between Bart and Al, those two keep me going. I've got to go."

"Yeah, I am certain things will be just fine for you."

Pat left my department, but no sooner did she get to the front end than her pager went off again.

Beep . . . beep . . . beep . . . beep . . . beep. "Pat, call extension 3651, Bob. She stopped at the front of the line, picked up the telephone and in an angry fashion yelled into the phone, "Be patient! I'm trying to do whatever I can to find you people to run your area completely." She then descended into the pressroom.

This time I managed to justify not giving up any of my people since the manufacturing requirements I was responsible for were of priority as well. Giving up any of my people to go to another work area would only cause my production to suffer; I am sure it would be held against me at some future date as a performance problem. I had to make certain that everything was perfect at all times. I did not have the same comfort or flexibility with General Motors as I did prior to filing charges against them. Wilbert's feedback and some of the other employees' comments were correct. I was a political hot potato, an outcast of the company as a direct result of filing charges against them.

However, there was no turning back at this time. There could be no regrets, even if the company chose not to resolve the conflict internally. I was the intruder in their area of corporate litigation, and they were equipped with a host of legal representatives both internally and externally, since they had litigated similar cases over the course of many years.

For the next few months I continued to run my department without incident. There were no production, quality or people problems at all. However, my nuts remained in General Motors' huge industrial vice. The corporation was unyielding in their efforts to collect any kind of information to use against me. I could tell without question that General Motors had been here before with regard to orchestrating an assault on an adversary. I just knew it would be a matter of time before I would be terminated, regardless of what I did. I knew my career was permanently damaged. Regardless of this fact, my work efforts were one hundred and fifty percent. I contributed constant and consistent improvements to the operations.

The next day I notified Pat of the problems we would encounter if inventory levels between the pressroom and Section One of my department were not maintained at optimum levels.

"Pat, I just wanted you to be aware that the inventory levels between the pressroom and Section One of my department are not adequate as a result of the production problems you had in the pressroom. Eventually it's going to bump my department. We've been running consistently well for months and months . . . ."

"Gary, I know the pressroom has been having a lot of problems. The people upstairs are all over me on it. Do whatever you can to keep going. Of course, you know I'm not going to stop until I run everything between the pressroom and my department. From the looks of things this evening, I am going to bump on requirements before lunch. If my crew of people are as motivated to work as they were last night, chances are we will bump before the first break."

"I'll keep you posted, but remember when it comes down to my appraisal, don't give me someone else's. I have not had any production, quality or people problems. In fact, my production has been extremely high. We have plenty of inventory between my department and final assembly, enough lead time for at least eight days of running without producing a single unit."

"I hope you're right on that, Gary."

"I know I am. Just look at the inventory reports, Pat. You'll see I'm correct. You know, there may be a chance you could have some of my people to help the other managers in the plant with their operations. However, I'd rather keep my people together because I could work on other assignments. Hold on, Pat. There's my driver. Eric, bring me everything out of the pressroom for these part numbers. We're running close, but I need to see everything we have between us. These inventories may be off."

"Okay, Boss."

"Pat, I have to go. I'll keep you fully informed of what happens. From the looks of things in the pressroom it appears as if they still have problems with those dies on the 1800 ton presses. I can see from here they are nesting them into the equipment. If I were you, I would get another tool and die and machine repairman on that equipment right now."

"I have a call in now for them."

"Well, call them again to make sure those presses can run all night. As you can see, my department is running and not missing any strokes. Those machines are doing just fine."

Pat began walking to the pressroom. She displayed a deep, dismal concern as she continued her walk towards the 1800 ton presses. I directed my efforts once again to all my responsibilities, making certain everything was completed as required. My days were stiff numbered. It was just a matter of time before GM authorities determined my fate.

"Wayne, Ricky, Richard, Ed, let's keep that equipment going, guys. Helen, Barbara, see if you can go through these parts and give us the best ones you have in each tub for the line, okay?"

"Sure, Gary."

"Eric, look we're down to half a basket in form of the department. We're going to bump just before break. G to Line Three; set that up. Let me know what we actually have in inventory for that line. Get it ready, Wayne, Ricky, go set up Line Three now. We only have about 15 minutes of production left on Line One."

"Okay," they replied.

It was a pleasure to hear the sounds of Line Three, as it appeared there were no equipment problems.

"Eric, put everything you have in from of the line. According to my reports, we're low on units for this part as well. Damn it. What's happening here? There's not a lot of surge here either. I am just going to run. I can't afford not to." The company would have my balls anyway they could. I was not going to give them that chance. The ball was in their court now. I have a job to do and couldn't sit still, not ever for a minute.

"We just bumped on parts. Line Three is down," said Eric.

"Well have ten minutes before lunch. Listen up people. Let's clean up the area. We have a little housekeeping to do in the department. Let's see that it's done."

"Oh, hi Wilbert."

"Hey, Gary. What's going on up here?"

"Nothin'. Just a little short. Hold on. I have to inform Pat of what we're dong. Okay, people, it's lunch time. Report back to Line Three when you're done. Thanks."

"Pat, we're bumped on parts. My entire line is down. Can we help run other lines or departments? What do you have?"

"Look, those damned presses are still down. I can't talk now. I'm talking to Bart."

"I understand, but you're sitting on the entire plan. I need to know where else you're having problems o we can help you. We're already run everything between my department and the pressroom."

"Not now, damn it! Bart . . . ! he's . . . ! Not now!"

"Pat, listen to me. We need to run . . . ."

"Run Line Two, damn it!"

"Pat, we can't run Line Two."

"I said run Line Two! Now run it!"

"Wilbert, listen to her! Pat, you can't run Line Two. It's totally apart for maintenance reasons."

"Just run Line Two! I said run Line Two . . . ! Bart . . . I can't talk. I have to go.

"What's wrong with her? The fucking line is completely torn apart and the power is locked out. What the fuck?"

"Damn, Wilbert, did you hear that?"

He grinned. "Heh heh, yeah, I heard her. She's up front with Bart in her office. Yeah I know, I just came from up there. She's steaming. They're at each others throats. She doesn't hear what the fuck you're saying."

"The line is completely torn apart. Who the fuck does pat think I am . . . Houdini? I know I'm good, but Line Two is completely disassembled. I wanted to tell her to run Lines Five and Six with my people through lunches and break. They have plenty of inventory."

"They definitely have their foot in her ass about this one."

"Who does, Wilbert?"

"The people upstairs. She's getting her ass kicked over this one."

"I can imagine."

"David, West, Carl, Fred, turn on the EBs. Bill, Woody, clear the exit conveyor on B Room. Let's go."

One month later I was given my appraisal by Pat in the main conference room of the plant.

"I hope you went lightly on me, Pat. As you know, I've completed all my assignments."

"Well, the way I rated you is good, competent in some areas, and needs improvement in others."

"I've done everything there was and completed all schedules and other assignments. Your appraisal is not correct. It's not a true rating of what I did."

"Well I do see you as a two rating (highly effective), but I have to eat, too, Gary. Damn it, my career is on the line."

"Yeah, I know what you mean, but it's not as nearly on the line as mine. In fact, my career is over simply because of filing the charges against the company, isn't it Pat?"

"I don't know, Gary, but I do know I have to eat. You do understand? By the way, a decision was made to transfer you to work on days with Eric Littrup."

"Who?"

"You know Littrup. Eric, who used to work in Shipping."

"What? I'm gong to the Shipping Department now?"

"No. Eric is in Manufacturing, Section Three. You know, your old stomping grounds."

"Yeah, what line do I have?"

"Well, I think they mentioned Line Six."

"You mean the manual operation?"

"Well, the units are not highly automated and damn near hand made."

"I only wish you could have been truthful about my performance, Pat"

"I did the best I could, Gary."

"Thanks, Pat. Take care. It's just a matter of time now before General Motors fires me. You know that's the reason for gradually lowering my appraisal from highly effective or outstanding rating to what you are giving me."

"No, you're mistaken."

"I don't think so, Pat. I will continue to give my best. You know I don't have the same support from the company any longer."

"I don't know about that Gary."

"Take care."

"Yeah, Gary. I will. You too."

The following week I began working with Eric Littrup in Section Three for the plant.

"Mr. McKnight. Hey, Mr. McKnight"

"Yeah? How are you doing Mike? I haven't seen you in quite some time. I guess it must have been sometime back in 1979 when I was in Building Three, running the special operation and the re-op department, correct?"

"Yea. It has been some time, but I did see you a couple times as you were going into the administrative offices. By the way, I hear you're to be working with Eric Littrup's group in Building Two Section Three of the plant."

"That's what they tell me. Where is he anyway? I didn't see him when I came in. I was up front in his office waiting for at least 25 minutes."

"I think he's on Line Five Section Three across from the line you're going to be running."

"Is that right? How did you know what line I was going to be assigned to? You're not a part of management."

"Mr. McKnight, you know we have our way of finding out things even before you guys."

"I know you have access to information. I'm just trying to get you to tell me your source and any other information you may have about what's going around here."

"You know I can't do that. But one thing I would do for you, my friend."

"What's that, Mike?"

"Keep you informed Mr. McKnight."

"Oh, Mike, by the way, call me Gary."

"Okay, Mr. McKnight, but just watch yourself."

"You know me, Mike. I always do. I am very careful about what I do around here."

"Oh, one other thing, Mr. McKnight. You're days with General Motors are numbered. Stay clear of Littrup. As I understand it, he's the one who's going to do you in. yep, you'd better watch it, buddy. I've got to go."

"Go ahead. But Mike? Remember, I don't miss a stroke. I do my fucking job to the fullest and you know that."

"Yeah, we all know it but it doesn't mean a thing and you know it. The company is out to get you for filing a lawsuit of some kind, and they are plenty fucking upset with you for doing. Besides, you were considered one of their company men, team player, one of their best. You surprised them with what you did."

"Let me tell you something. I cannot confirm what you're saying, but I will say this. I have no fucking choice. Let's just leave it at that. Take care my friend."

"Okay, Mr. McKnight."

"Please, just call me Gary."

Damn! I was certain what Mike was saying was correct. I'd been informed by employees throughout the plant about my ordeal and General Motors' plans to terminate me and end my career. However, I just could not confirm their thoughts. I simply would not go into the details of this bout with General Motors. I was in it. They started it and I was determined to remain in contention with them as long as necessary. I would no be intimidated by anyone. Although my career was gone at this point, I continued to deliver and performed my responsibilities at all times. I knew for certain I didn't have the support of the company on my side. This only made my job more difficult.

I knew for a fact what Mike said had to be coming from a reliable source. It's not at all unusual at General Motors to receive sensitive information from members of management who are in the know, even though the informants are not members management.

"Hey, Cal. Where are you working?"

"Line Six . . . same department as you. Part is yours and part is mine."

"I've noticed there's been a frequent turnover in workers. Am I correct?"

"Yeah, that's correct"

"What's the problem?"

"They just don't like the area and everything else that comes with it. It's a very difficult area. It requires constant supervision."

"Well, I can see why. It's not the best equipment in the world, or for that matter, in plant."

"You're one hundred percent right. At first, some people think it's Hillbilly Heaven' when they see it, but once they attempt their first run they're ready to get out of the fucking area in a wee."

"What? You have to be kidding."

"You'll see. We're constantly changing the line over to run several different requirement, compared to the other lines that may change over only several times in a year. We're doing it several times week and sometimes a day."

"Yeah, I know. I'm familiar with the department. By the way, Cal, where's Eric Littrup," I asked. "I have to talk with him."

"Last I saw him, about a half hour ago, he was on Line Five, knee deep in a shitload of problems," Cal responded.

"Cal, who's running that line, anyway?"

"Barry, a couple of engineers and whoever else they could get over there."

"Including Littrup as well, I guess," I added.

"Well, you may be right. They've been having problems for quite some time now, and Eric has been over there now for quite a while."

"I see Barry got a promotion into management since I've been gone form the area."

"Yeah, you're right. He did get promoted from hourly. But you'll have your problems, McKnight, soon enough."

"I guess it's how you see it, Cal."

"You'll see it all right. Just wait."

"Well, I'm here to get the job done," I said. Then, "Hey, Eric, are you in position to talk?"

Eric shook his head with no frown. "Not now." His face had an expression of tremendous frustration, as if his head were about to explode. His eyes protruded as he crossed his arms firmly across his chest. Although he appeared angered, he remained speechless as he and the engineers gathered around the troubled equipment. He continued to motion his head up and down with a very angry expression.

Barry constantly took drags on his cigarette, one after the other, as did Littrup, as they watched the engineers attempt to locate the needed tooling, hoping this would finally solve the problem. Not running many parts on Line Five continues for weeks and months. The products coming off the line could not have met production standards at all.

Given Eric's preoccupation with the problems on Line Five, I had time to study the routings for my department in order to understand the productive requirements of Line Six.

Even though I knew my relationship with General Motors Corporation was superficial at this time, I have to be prepared and make certain everything I did was perfect regarding production schedules and quality standards. I new from the very beginning that General Motors was returning me to this environment to completely change my outstanding performance appraisals to substandard one, laying the groundwork for my termination. At this time, regardless of what I did for General Motors, the company wanted to terminate for the mere fact I filed charged and a lawsuit against them.

Although several other managers for the company were having major productive difficulties, it was considered a performance problem, and they would not be terminated by General Motors.

In any given industrial environment, managers will be confronted with manufacturing difficulties. The problems which develop are common and recurring. However, in my situation, I was not having problems meeting schedules at all. In fact, all my product requirements were completed on schedule with high quality all the time. Up until now, I have completed all scheduled requirements without incident or customer complaints from either our Allied Divisions (divisions within General Motors) or our Non-Allied Divisions (customer outside GM). However, the appraisals I was given upon my reassignment to the manufacturing group were completely false because the work was being done. This, of course, did not mean anything to General Motors. It was just a matter of time before they terminated me. Quite simply, my career with GM. I was considered an adversary by the company and was working without their support. General Motors was building their case against me even as I worked for them. Periodically, I say groups of outsiders into the plant where the manufacturing activity was held, observing the operations of my area and other sections. Although several may have been outside vendors, I sensed some of the visitors had other interests in mind. Genera Motors' lawyers, at this time, had several advantages over me. They could observe me without my knowing who they were. They could have the company give me difficult assignments, create production difficulties, encourage others to testify against me and attempt to use that information as evidence against me later in courts. These were very significant advantages.

I knew it would be difficult for me to have others testify against General Motors, however, I had to make certain information which reflected what I actually contributed to General Motors was presented. I did not think General Motors would say these things about my performance in open court if they held into my accomplishments as documented in writing. Therefore, I made photo copies of my original documented work assignments before I turned them over.

Any competent lawyer should do tremendously well with the evidence of my work performance, if it came down to actually litigating these issues. The mere fact I was telling the truth was enough to convince me our legal system can work. Only time would show the reality of how our legal system handled the issues to be resolved between myself and General Motors.

"Hi Sylvia, Gladys," I said as they walked past me with a slight not of their heads.

"Mr. McKnight, Mr. McKnight," rang out over the sound levels of the surrounding manufacturing operating equipment. It was a trucker named John Nason.

"Yeah? How can I help you?" I replied.

"Mr. McKnight, where would you like me to put this material?"

"Put it in the payroll area. You've only two baskets."

"Okay, Mr. McKnight"

"John, call me Gary. Thanks."

"Okay, Boss."

"John, after you put the two baskets in the payroll area (end of the production line for shipping and final inventory). I need you to completely strip the line and bring me the materials for this product requirement. We are going to completely change this line over in order to run Isuzus. I only want the best materials on this line of our customers.

"Will do, Boss," John replied.

"Thanks, John," replied, "Let's go, people. I'm your assigned manager. I guess you know that by now. I'm certain you are familiar with what your responsibilities are."

"Yes," the group responded.

"However, I am certain you can give a little bit more than what you have in the past. I have studied the results on this line and I am certainly not used to the levels of units produced here. They seem kind of low to me."

"Well, this line is not the other lines. However, it is important for you to understand that we have to give more in order to stay competitive in the automotive industry. If we do not do all we can, eventually we will lose our competitiveness. We will lose our customer," I said. "Thank you for your attention. I need you to set up your work area. We will be building the Isuzu units for shipment to Japan. Let's work smarter and safer, people," I added.

"Mr. McKnight," John call. "I completely cleared the line of the material that was before and replaced it with the new material for the Isuzu."

"Okay, good," I said.

"Hey, Mr. McKnight, I just want you to know this is considered one of the most difficult areas to manage and it's been said this line has broken managers who have worked it before. It will keep you hopping. There's never a dull moment here," said John.

"Well, I'm not concerned about that, John. I have a job to do and I am going to do it," I said.

"I know, but watch yourself. What I'm saying is just be careful," John said.

"I'm always careful, John, but thanks for the advice. I can see you are concerned. I need some additional units for my people. I need you to take care of that. Thanks," I said.

Several weeks passed and I continued on a daily basis to run every unit produced by the crew ahead of me, meeting production schedules ahead of time for the next changeover. I continued pacing the floor of the industrial environment under the sounds of thundering machines. I carefully monitored production and performance 'of my people, often making certain that everything was going well, it went perfectly. The quality was there, and there were no complaints or returns from our customers. However, due to the impending litigation against General Motors, I still knew things were not going to the same as they were before. I felt I could have run General Motors Corporation itself with a little help, however, nothing mattered to GM other than their legal involvement with me. I was willing and determined to finish what was started if General Motors could not come to a resolution internally.

Indeed, I continued doing my job, often pacing the floor, working non-stop. My clothing reeked, soaked with my body's sweat which often dripped onto the plant floor. I continued walking back and forth in the areas which required close frequent management supervision because of the design and staffing of some of the company's oldest machinery. It was extremely important to focus on my responsibilities and not give General Motors anything significantly tangible to use against me as evidence to support their position in court. Quite simply, I knew General Motors was going to terminate me eventually and was going to use the falsely created assertions in the appraisals against me. However, I remained focused on my work.

Each day I noticed other managers throughout the plant having various manufacturing problems. Several of these problems came out during our management meeting. My operations were non-eventful, running smoothly each day. It was my objective to stay out of the grasp of management and any criticisms they attempted to create. In addition, I wanted to avoid Erip Littrup. From the way he looked at me at times it appeared he would kill me if he had the chance. He spent most of his time working with the other managers on Lines Five and Four, who were having significant down time. However, theses mangers were not censored, or even terminated, for their performance. Instead, some were promoted.

I tried to limit myself in conversation with Eric Littrup, who never openly complained about my performance. However, at special appraisal times, he would cite negative comments which were unfounded. I did the best I could, meeting schedules, maintaining quality and satisfying my customers. The company could not have asked for anything more from me, other than for me to consider signing the waiver of release of the charges, and Bonnie did that often. I new eventually even Eric Littrup would try to create a situation that he would perhaps be able to use against me.

On one occasion, Eric approached me and said, "Gary, I was going through your area at lunch time and noticed Judy didn't have her safety glasses on. She may have been reading on the line. I want you to fire her."

I said, "Fire her? What do you mean fire her? She has been doing a good job for me, so far."

"Well, she's in violation of company policy and I want you to fire her," Eric said.

"Well, Eric, you the authority to recommend she be fired, however, there are several steps you must go through first before you can just fire her. In my opinion, nothing supports terminating her just like that. Generally, I have a discussion with the employee and try to find out what the problem is. If it is going to repeat itself, I involve their Union representative as well as our Personnel people," I said.

"I said fire her," Eric demanded.

"Listen, Eric. Those individuals I determine should be placed on probation, disciplined or fired, I do myself," I said. "Now, when an employee violates company policy there are certain procedures to follow. For me to simply do as you are suggesting would cause problems for me with the company and the Union, not to mention that it would not be fair for her. Eric, you are going to have to take me upstairs on this one because it's simply not right. The issue of her not wearing glasses I will dismiss with her. Now are you giving me a direct order to fire Judy?"

There was no response. Eric turned and sucked in his lips, shaking his head from side to side. He looked flustered and his face turned bright red. He definitely was angry by my decision not to terminate Judy.

Several weeks went by and I continued to do tremendous job meeting schedules, building product requirements to print, and maintaining customer satisfaction. I continued pacing the shop floor in the huge industrial facility of General Motors, making certain everything went well. At the same time, my wife was expecting our third child. What a time for her to get pregnant, but life goes on.

At the close of the shift I received a phone call from Eric asking if I could cone in early to run a crew of people since the schedules were picking up and our customers wanted more units than they ordinarily ordered.

I said, "Sure. If the company needs more units, I'll come in early." This would be 2:00 in the morning, part of third shift operations. First shift started at 6:30 in the morning.

Everything seemed to be going well. Production was steady, people were in order. I needed more catalyst. "Where's my driver? Where's my catalyst tote?"

The driver said, "It hasn't been released yet, Boss."

"What? Not released? Where's the quality guy who is responsible for releasing it?"

"I last saw him on the back end of Line Four, going toward Line Three," the driver said.

"Well, I have to get him to release that catalyst tote now before my line bumps," I said. "Tell him I said I need that tote cleared now, or my line is going down."

"He's not going to listen to me. You know that Mr. McKnight."

"Well let me go get him. You just keep an eye out for the other needs of the line, okay?"

"Yeah, okay," the driver said.

This whole area was cluttered with material. What the hell was going on here? I walked through the opening in the conveyor of Line Five, an approved walkthrough. I could see that catalyst tote approval person from here.

No sooner had I cleared the opening in the conveyor and stepped out to walk further. Then suddenly and precipitously without warning, a forklift truck weighing several hundred pounds was coming in my direction. All at once I heard the rumbling, thundering sound of the forklift and manufacturing equipment and saw a quick flash of the blades attempt to pierce whatever portion of my body it could catch. The blades miraculously positioned above my two feet and as I pushed off the truck to keep from falling in the path of destruction, I say the faces of three people quickly flash before my. My body miraculously maneuvered to avoid an injury that would have been permanent.

As I pushed off the truck and into the moving conveyor, I say Eric Littrup look in my direction and suddenly turn his head and walk among the 55-gallon drums at the back of Line Five.

Eric turned his head and walked away as if he didn't notice. I caught the face of the driver. It was Chuck Cronk, the brother of Denis Cronk, one of the managers who had harassed me. This was quite a coincidence, indeed.

The fork truck continued its thrust forward traveling at such a speed as to do significant damage to anyone or anything in its path. As I managed to pull myself together and off the conveyor, I immediately summoned the driver, "Hey, Chuck. Stop your vehicle, now! Do you realize you almost hit me?"

"Huh? Who, me? I didn't see you. I mean, you walked in front of me as I was coming through the area," Chuck said.

"Well, don't you know you have an obligation to drive your vehicle safely in a heavy pedestrian area of the plant?"

"But I . . . I didn't see you until I was right on top of you," he said.

"Then, why did you keep going?"

"I stopped eventually," he said.

"Yeah, I see that . . . several feet ahead," I said. "Listen, Chuck. I'm putting a call in for Fred."

"Fred? Who's Fred?" Chuck asked.

"Fred LeBlanc. Isn't he your manager? After all, this is his area," I said.

"No, I report to Paul Huberty," Chuck replied.

"Well, I want you to know I will have to contact him as well as your Union representative, and our plant safety director, Bob."

"For what? What have I done?" Chuck asked.

"First of all, you have been involved in a near-miss accident involving a pedestrian, namely me. And even if it wasn't me, I would do the same thing for any other employee of the company."

"You can't do this," Chuck said.

"Listen, mister. You are hereby placed on notice for possible disciplinary action pending an investigation of the events which have just occurred and any other such occurrences."

"Like hell I am. My brother is Denis Cronk. You're not going to do anything to me," Chuck said.

"Maybe that's your problem, not mine," I said. "You are on formal notice and will be given written notice of this incident."

"Gary, you had someone call me?" Paul asked.

"Yeah, I called you," I said. "I need you to put Chuck on notice as a result of a near-miss accident involving a pedestrian . . . me . . . pending an investigation of the event in order to make it official," I said.

"I don't know if I can do that," Paul said.

"Of course, you can. Just ask him if he was involved in a near-miss accident. If he confirms, then you put him on notice and I will handle the details," I said.

"If you say so," Paul said.

"Well, if you don't want to do it, get your boss down here and I'll look into this further myself. If it was simply an accident, then I will leave it at that."

"What about the paperwork, Gary? Who's going to do the paperwork?" Paul asked.

"What paperwork? You can take that paperwork and shove it!" Chuck said.

"What did you say? Get down off that truck now! I am giving you a direct order. Move it. I want you up front now," I said.

Eventually, Eric Littrup, the General Manager of Production, and several others were involved in the discussions of the near-miss accident and Chuck

Cronk's performance. People from Labor Relations in Personnel were there, too. After tempers cooled off a bit, we left it that Chuck would get a warning this time and it would be considered further to become a part of his work record. It was a miracle I was not seriously injured, escaping with just some contusions on my side.

I regained my composure and continued with my responsibilities. In fact, I never really lost myself in terms of handling the situation professionally. I just had to resort to a management technique using the tell method in order to contain the situation between Chuck and myself.

"Gary," called voices from a distance above the thundering sounds of the heavy operating equipment.

"Hey, Wilbert. How are you doing, Bill?" I asked.

"We're okay. How about yourself? We heard you were almost injured," they said.

"Maybe. Maybe not. Now guys, later," I said. I immediately informed my attorney, Mark, of the incident between Chuck Cronk and myself and of Chuck's relationship to Denis. I also informed the officials from the Department of Labor and Industry. They reassured me they would look into the incident during their involvement.

Later that evening, my wife and I dined out at a fine restaurant in the area. The evening was going rather well.

"Gary, what's wrong? How come you're so quiet?" my wife asked.

"Oh, it's nothing, really," I said.

"Come on. I can see you are thinking about something else," she said.

"Yeah, you're right," I admitted. "I don't know how to explain this, but I'll try. Today at work I was involved in a near-miss vehicle accident with Denis Cronk's brother, Chuck," I said.

"Chuck Cronk? Are you sure it was an accident?" she questioned.

"Well, I'm not entirely sure," I replied. "Chuck and his truck were right on top of me. I went through the conveyor opening and the next thing I knew this forklift truck was there right on top of me. Somehow, I managed to get out of its way. The only thing I can recall is pushing away from it," I said.

"I went back to the area to examine what happened and discovered there was a blind spot for the pedestrian, but not the driver. If you are the driver of the forklift, you can see all moving pedestrian traffic in the plant. However, my vision was restricted because of the weld booth next to the line by the opening in the conveyor. I'm not certain if Chuck Cronk deliberately timed my travel through the opening or if I just could not see him because of the weld booth, but suddenly, there he was, right on me. I hope it was just an accident," I said.

"Why don't you just get out of there?" Shirley asked.

"Shirley, I'm a family man. I need to support a wife and two kids, and another on the way. It's just not that easy. Although my request for a transfer to another

General Motors facility has been processed through Personnel, they said Detroit would have to decide whether I would be transferred or not. My request has been made several times. Hopefully they will transfer me back to the New York-New Jersey area," I said. "I am certain, though, that General Motors is moving ahead with these plans to eventually terminate my employment."

"You really know how to make me feel secure, don't you?" Shirley said.

"Hell, I guess so. I can't tell General Motors what to do. I'm certain they've been here before," I said.

"Good evening, Mr. and Mrs. McKnight. Are you ready to order?" the waiter asked after giving us some time.

"Yes," we agreed.

Several weeks passed. I continued producing at an even greater rate and with very high levels of customer satisfaction.

Regardless of my good performance and contributions to General Motors, as measured by my high production and quality standards, Eric Littrup continued paving the way for my termination. He was unyielding in regard to finishing what the other manager appraisals of me had started. Indeed, this was a well orchestrated plan.

Eric Littrup was just another person involved in the process of my termination. He would perhaps make the final decision. He seemed to be the main player in this conspiracy to terminate me. However, I was certain he was not the main player behind the corporation's efforts. It appeared as if he enjoyed being a part of the process.

Their plan of termination could almost be compared to that of a conspiracy to murder. After all, Eric Littrup was working for Denis Cronk, who was one of the named defendants in the lawsuit I filed.

Regardless of my knowledge about their plan to eventually terminate my employment in complete disregard of my actual performance, I continued doing my job with evidence of very high standards of production. However, nothing could stop General Motors' plans to go forward with my scheduled termination. The writing had been on the wall for some time now. It was not only apparent to me, but had been known to others for some time now.

My third daughter was born in September of 1983. This brought some happiness to my life as her birth helped take my mind off the way I was being treated at work. This pleasure would be short lived.

There was one other employee I had to manage closely and give a formal notice of reprimand. This individual was transferred to my department and did not want to work as productively as the others. After two verbal warnings, the unacceptable work performance on his part affected others. And General Motors' Labor Relations group had assigned the employee to my department.

The employee eventually admitted to being wrong and disruptive and asked that I give him a chance and spare his job, since his employment history with General Motors was not good. Any additional formal discipline would have required the employee to be put on the street, even though most often it seems as if a Union worker is difficult to fire permanently. It appeared as if the company could permanently fire the Chairman or any member of General Motors' management before they could a Union worker.

Each day I continued pacing the floor and handling all my responsibilities throughout. The sweat continued pouring from my body. Often I would be required to manage several additional productive operations at the same time, and it would not even be considered by the company. In effect, this treatment was a form of pure, unadulterated harassment, because I was required to do it but was not given any credit or recognition for it.

Eric Littrup briefly indicated he had placed me on a performance improvement plan and that the time was up. He was determined to carry out the plan to eliminate my position. He appeared cold and inconsiderate of anything I said in regard to my performance.

I told Eric he was being tremendously unfair, that his assertions were not true of my actual performance and that his comments were injurious to my career. I also indicated to him that I was being treated differently.

Shortly afterward, I was called to Eric Littrup's office and went upstairs to the administrative building of the General Motors Corporation. Eric, Bonnie and Tom were present. The Personnel Manager and the Director of Manufacturing were not. They had several documents for me to sign. I refused to sign most of them, agreeing to sign only the document informing me of my termination.

"Eric, I would like to know the reason for my termination," I requested.

"Performance," Eric replied.

"Performance?" I asked.

"Yeah, performance," Eric said.

"Mr. McKnight, do you have anything to say?" Tom asked.

"Call me Gary, Tom," I said. "The only thing I have to say is that what you're doing here is unfair and I do not agree with it. I did my job. The decision is yours. That's all I can say."

"Well, we must inform you that at the end of the shift today your employment with General Motors will terminate for reasons of performance," Eric said.

"I understand. Here's my time card and employee identification badge. Have a good day, gentlemen." As I walked out of the office I was greeted by several people who had either worked for me or with me. They all seemed to come at once. However, I nodded my head as a friendly gesture and continued my brisk walk through the administration building, through the industrial manufacturing facility, to my desk and through to the plant exit.

Then I heard, "Gary, hold on."

I stopped and looked back. It was Eric Littrup. "Yeah?" I said.

"Hold on. I am supposed to escort you out of the plant," Eric said.

"That's okay, Eric. I know my way out," I replied.

"Well, it's company policy. Do you have anything else to say, Gary?" Eric asked.

"Yeah, take care, Eric. Take care," I said.

As I departed through the security gate and turned towards the area of the parking lot where my car was located, I saw Eric still standing with both hands on his hips and a look of despair on his face.

It was a clear day in the month of November, 1983. As I arrived home I continued my normal daily routine as if nothing had happened. During dinner I informed my wife of my termination from General Motors.

"Hon, let's go to bed," my wife suggested.

CHAPTER IV

Tomorrow's Future

The next day I began looking for work elsewhere. Also, I notified my attorney and the Department of Labor and Industry, giving them all the details, leading up to and including my termination. I asked them to pursue all issues which could be litigated and not limit it to employment, as there may be issues of defamation and tort claims, as well as entitlements under Title VII, a congressional statute approved in 1964 by the U.S. Congress and now Federal law. I was assured these matters would be handled.

My employment search continued for several months without success. In February of 1984 I was once again provided the opportunity to go on additional job interviews. Merrill Lynch, a Wall Street related investment firm also noted to be one of the most prestigious and premiere financial investment houses, was one of my prospective employers.

Placement with the investment firm of Merrill Lynch was not right away. I continued my search primarily with manufacturing and financial organizations, but I also used a broad employment approach just in case nothing turned up similar to the jobs at General Motors, as the country was slipping further into a recession.

Throughout this period, I pressed my attorney, Mark, for settlement of my claims against the huge General Motors Corporation, including but not limited to the following: getting my job back, being transferred to another General Motors facility out of state, settling those entitlements known under Title VII, and any other entitlements under other legal statutes pursuant to the operants of the United States Supreme Court. I was also open to consideration of alternative settlement arrangements to compensate for the injuries to my person. My attorney assured me he would pursue all claims and negotiate with General Motors Corporation to come to some kind of agreement.

"Mark, you know it's important that you go over the facts of my case very thoroughly. There may be other claims here I missed, and I'd greatly appreciate it if you could explore those other areas as well," I suggested.

"I know, Gary. After all that's why you've hired the best attorney in Milwaukee," Mark said.

"Well, my objective here is to get my job back and be removed from a hostile environment. Since General Motors Corporation is so large, they should not have a problem making that arrangement, as well as seeing that I get all my lost benefits and other entitlements. You know I was previously called back to General Motors by their personnel representative some time in February of this year to consider negotiating an arrangement with the company concerning this litigation. However, before we could continue our discussions they wanted me to drop my attorney. When I told them I was under contract with you and could not do that, they wanted to end all discussions. They later indicated I could speak with their director in Detroit, Michigan, but only if I dropped you. I asked Phil to have him contact you, or have their local attorneys contact you instead."

"Before I left the General Motors facility, Phil, the Personnel Manager, demanded I turn over the photo copied of my work documents, which proved I had done my job. Indeed, my termination of employment was wrongful."

"Good Gary," attorney Mark said.

"Keep in mind, Mark, that I'm out of work and in need of immediate substantial work. I have three kids to provide for, and a wife. This involvement could hurt me."

"I know, Gary," Mark said.

After several extensive interviews and testing with Merrill Lynch, I was finally placed with them in April of 1984. although I initially interviewed for, and requested to go into management, investment banking and corporate finance. I was offered a position as a retail account executive, financing consultant pursuing individual and corporate clients for investment matters. This resulted in a substantial compensation loss for me and my family compared to what I had earned at General Motors. However, the earning potential at Merrill Lynch, I began developing significant investment relationships. It appeared to begin to pay off, but then Merrill Lynch got wind of my legal involvement with General Motors, although I had never talked to anyone whatsoever about it. However, my quest with General Motors was unyielding. I was often summoned for legal depositions and to answer interrogatives.

CHAPTER V

Trials and Tribulations

In January of 1986, shortly following the McKnight vs. General Motors trial held in the state of Wisconsin Circuit Court, and subsequent to Mark handling that case, I had to go forward with all that remained. It appeared as if Mark was uncertain regarding the posture of the case, and I was very disappointed with the developments and the outcome of the Circuit Court Trial. Although it had taken a long time to get to trial following the initial filing of the charges before the Labor Department, there seemed not to have been any meaningful settlement discussion that I was aware of, though I knew my settlement terms were quire significant.

Given the GM did not respond favorably to any meaningful settlement terms and discussions, I thought it was best to allow my attorney to litigate all relevant issued before all administrative and legal forums. Quite simply, this is how I ended up in State Court in Wisconsin before a Circuit Court jury. The jury was asked to determine, by a special verdict question format approved by the Circuit Court Judge, whether General Motors' conduct was extremely outrageous and egregious. Although I had vehemently asked my attorney to object to that question and format as inappropriate, the question went to the jury anyway.

The jury came back with a finding of compensatory damages of $75,000 and $5,000 in miscellaneous expenses. The presiding judge ruled that in this particular case the issue of punitive damages would not be allowed as it was not appropriate. Now keep in mind, the issue of punitive damages was not considered by the jury because certain requirements are necessary for it to be an issue. Implicitly, we did not meet that requirement so it was not for the jury to consider. Yet, at the same time, the presiding Circuit Court judge approved the question format to include "Was the defendant General Motors' conduct extremely outrageous and egregious?" these terms are generally used in murder trials.

I thought if such terms were to be used in my civil trial with General Motors, and if the jury said yes, then punitive damages should have gone before the jury. So here we have a State Court jury establishing damages of approximately $80,000 without consideration of punitive damages, and I, the plaintiff, cannot collect this award due to a defect in the special verdict.

Keep in mind, I had already been substantially damaged by the conditions of employment I was subjected to, especially after I filed be grievances. Malicious assertions against me, though, were later retracted through subsequent testimony of expert witnesses.

Although I was capable of behaving differently or unacceptably, I did not. With the help of God and a little bit of belief in the legal system, I was able to maintain my composure. However, as each day went by I grew less and less composed, but I managed to maintain a respectful level of professionalism. It was extremely important for me to conduct myself as a gentleman at all times, but that was me anyway, it's the way I've been since as early as I can remember. However, at time when I did have to engage in strife, I had to get rough with the opponent.

In a courtroom there is no tolerance at all for those who lose their composure. There's even a good chance that if you look at the judge the wrong way, although you're the injured party, you may be found in contempt of court and thrown in jail. You certainly have to be careful.

As I reflected back on the Sate Court trial which occurred in December of 1985, and listened to the false assertions against me which were later dispelled by expert testimony, I thought I was blessed by God. It was very important for me to have my attorney take charge of the situation both inside and outside the court room. By this time it appeared as if someone had a mission to deliberately create difficulty for me. What the hell did General Motors want with me? They certainly did not want me to become wealthy. I was highly motivated and on the road to becoming wealthy even before I was hired by GM. Even their representative indicated on several occasions that they hire the best, and they know that before you're hired. However, I doubted that because of the way I was treated and my career mishandled. I knew this, as did several other managers at General Motors. I did everything I could within corporate guidelines to salvage my career and get around the difficulties confronting me.

On numerous occasions I requested to be transferred to protect my career and keep highly effective to outstanding performance ratings so I could move upward, but to no avail. I ended up here in a courtroom in Wisconsin, a state with conservative values. It appeared as if the entire system had conservative opinions about the issues before it. This could actually be confirmed by the results. However, life goes on, and it could happen to someone else . . . maybe even you.

As you can gather, the process is not so simple and rather frustrating. It seemed as if the concepts of fairness and equity had been forgotten or circumvented altogether. The victim became more victimized as the process continues. Does the system work? Can it? What one gives the other takes. What one forgets the other remembers. Most often in this legal maze of uncertainty you must depend on your lawyer so no aspect of your case is jeopardized. However, at times you might want to temper his advice with your own judgment.

*   *   *

"Hello, law offices," the receptionist answered.

"Is attorney Mark in?"

"Yes he is. Who's calling. One moment please."

"Yeah, Gary, what can I do for you?" said Mark.

"That's a good question, Mark. Only you should already have the answer to that one, don't you think?"

"Well that depends on what you're calling about."

"I am calling about the appeal of my case before the trial judge. When are you going to appeal it, and do need me to further discuss any information with you about this legal movement?"

"I don't know. I haven't decided if it would do us any good to appeal this thing. I mean . . ."

"Hold on Mark. What do you mean you haven't decided if it would do us any good?"

"Can you let me finish, Gary? In most instances, appeals are more difficult to get overturned, although it's not impossible. I have to see if you have enough here to make an appeal worthwhile."

"I understand, but you don't have a lot of time to decide if you're going to appeal or not. Mark, as far as I am concerned, I'd like you to appeal this matter as soon as possible. If you haven't done so already, I'd like you to go before the trial judge and preserve all my legal entitlements for appeal."

"Gary, you don't . . ."

"Mark, maybe you haven't decided yet, but I have. Just appeal this matter as soon as possible. From a layman's point of view, there were several things that occurred with the jury I concluded were improver. Also, the jury came back with a judgment of approximately $80,000 in damages without the issue of punitive damages going before them. I think I should have been entitled to the punitives as well, and you know I took exception to the special verdict questions.

"The jury's conduct was not proper. Their comments indicated they thought the defendants treated me that way because I was 'uppity' and lived in a big fancy home in Greenfield. This is completely irrelevant to the defendant's conduct. My injuries and loss of reputation are the issued here. You know that. You don't treat someone that way because they have more qualifications or money than you. I certainly don't feel that way towards the Rockefellers or the Kennedys or, for that matter, anyone. No one should set out to deliberately injure someone because of who they are.

"Mark, it's important you get on this right away. You know I am not making as much as I did while working for GM. In the mean time, you may want to see if a settlement is possible with our opponents. If not, then you know what to do. Just go forward with the appeal. Okay, Mark?"

"I'll see, Gary."

As time passed, I felt it necessary to prepare for mark's withdrawal as I sensed a reluctance on his part to continue this litigation.

* * *

It was only a matter of time before the results of the trial got back to my colleagues at GM. I found it necessary, at least in my own right, to understand the significance of what alternatives I had left, this entire involvement with the State Court proceedings would be a total fiasco. Personally, I did not want to reach this conclusion yet, as I remained a strong believer in the legal system in America. Again, keep in mind this was most likely General Motor's turf anyway. There, one could easily conclude General Motors had s slight advantage over me in this regard.

At this point it really didn't matter to me that General Motors had many advantages. My motivation to continue the litigation was fueled by the mere fact that a deliberate wrong had been perpetrated against me and, ultimately, against my family. This I have never tolerated from anyone. Besides, I did not want this kind of treatment to happen to anyone so similarly situated.

During the continuation of this battle, I continued the development of my investment business with Merrill Lynch. It appeared as if my development was right on target. My retail business was doing rather well on a comparative basis, and I have established significant venture capital and corporate finance relationships which could potentially provide more in terms of compensation that what I had gained as a result of the State Court trial.

The transactions I developed were arrangements of multi-million dollar amounts. However, it was the principle of the matter. A bird in the hand is worth two in the bush.

Although I believe in being a team player, it seemed in both instances I had to do it alone. At Merrill Lynch I was involved in the arrangement of several venture capital matters which were promptly referred to our venture capital people for final approval as these kinds of arrangements were rather more speculative than the more traditional kind of corporate trading. Although I'm on John Delorean or Roger Smith, I can remember a particular venture capital request involving an automotive company which sold car kits and wanted to assemble and mass produce their model vehicle on a broader scale. Although I was aware of the tremendous difficulty in the development of the concept to mass produce their product, it was not entirely impossible given the right balance of things. If the principles were genuinely interested, I was certain we could arrange some sort of leveraged buy-out of an existing company. In addition, where were other significant transactions which were not of a venture capital nature, but of privately or publicly held companies. It takes time to complete these transactions.

It appeared as if my compensation were being contained in my respects. Most often it seemed that what I was involved in was orchestrated in such a way as to contain and curtail my economic development. What General Motors had done in the way of my compensation with them determined the damages to be approximately $80,000, which I was not able to collect due to a defect in the special verdict. Although I never talked to anyone at Merrill Lynch about my legal involvement, I knew it was inevitable they'd find out. It was just a matter of time.

*   *   *

"Mr. McKnight, Mr. Oglesby is on line two."

"Can he wait a minute? I have to finish this call with a client." A moment later I answered, "Wilbert, how can I help you?"

"Where's the market?"

"It's up 35 points so far and it's going higher."

"What are you recommending?"

"Walmart stores, Merck, Microsoft, Lowes, Time. Telephone looks good here and so does Pennzoil, IBM, Exxon and a few others. However, I'll have to look at the research before I encourage you to buy them. How many shares can I get you? What do you want?"

"Hey, McKnight, what the fuck happened to your State Court trial? Rumor has it you lost. How the hell did that happen?"

"Where did you hear that?"

"Bonnie, Gil and Eric were in a meeting. I guess General Motors' lawyers indicated to them that you lost."

"Lost? Not really."

"Then what happened? How could your lawyer allow get away with that one?"

"Well, Wilbert, the jury established damages of $80,000 in compensatory and other damages, but I couldn't collect due to a legal technicality, some sort of defect in the special verdict. And the issue of punitive damages was not allowed to go before the jury."

"Defect. Special verdict. What the fuck are you talking about? Why the hell would your lawyer have me come to court and not allow me to testify? The company may put their foot in my behind for this and I didn't even take the stand."

"That's a good question. I discussed this with him. I asked him to have several management people, as well as those who worked for me testify. Sometimes you have to let the attorney work his theory of the case. You can't tell him how to litigate. I mean, you shouldn't have to, anyway. Besides, that's why they went to law school. By the way, what were their reactions?"

"Hell, they were jumping for joy and laughing. They said their attorneys said they won."

"No, they didn't. Like I said before, due to a defect. I couldn't collect damages the jury determined. That means something is not right with the question is the special verdict. I am gong to appeal this thing."

"Appeal?"

"Yeah, appeal. It's just not right. If the jury establishes liability in the way of damages, then I win. But if my attorney allows a technicality to get by so I can't collect, then I guess the other side laugh. It's not over yet, though. I am going to appeal. General Motors knew I told the truth and I didn't say anything that didn't happen. Denis and Gil knew I told the truth."

"Well, personally, I think you lawyer was not very aggressive. He should have allowed me and a few others to testify on your behalf."

"Maybe next time. But maybe General Motors would have done something to you, too."

"They may do something to me for just showing up."

"Well you had to' you were subpoenaed, I still have to tell the wife and the kids that General Motors got away without paying the $80,000 in damages that the jury determined. I can see Eric, Gil, Denis and Bonnie going home and telling their families that although I told the truth, I didn't collect my damage award. They see this as a loss on my part. 'If they didn't believe McKnight, they won't believe a dead man either, now would they?' I just know what they are saying. It's not right, Wilbert"

"Mr. McKnight," called Linda.

"Yes?"

"New York is on line three. Mr. Pittman, Dr. Mari, Mr. Williams, and Mr. Morgan are on hold. Chicago wants you to call them."

Wilbert, I've got to go. Get back to me with your order. Hey, say hello to everyone back at the shop, will ya?"

CHAPTER VI

Changing of the Guards

By February of 1986, my confidence in Mark was questionable. I could not understand why he was not trying to get General Motors to dispose of this matter once and for all. I knew I had worked competently and conscientiously for General Motors, yet I could not understand how my career would suddenly take a turn for the worse. My confidence level was very high in terms of believing I could win this bout with General Motors. I even trusted and believed in Mark. I knew if I were the attorney representing a plaintiff against General Motors, I would have given it all until the very end.

However, something was definitely wrong here. Shortly following the State Court trial with General Motors, Mark indicated that our chances for getting the decision reversed or winning on appeal were not good.

"Gary, I haven't decided if I'm going to appeal this verdict yet. Our chances are not good."

"I don't understand, Mark. What are you saying?" I questioned.

"Well," he replied, "it's very difficult to win on appeal, and I don't know if we should continue. But I haven't made my final decision."

"Well, I need to know something from you soon because we don't have a lot of time to wait. I'd like you to tell me what you plan to do in the next few days because the way I see it, we can win this thing. Besides, there were a lot of questionable things that went on in that State Court trial which may be grounds for giving us a shot at a successful appeal."

"For instance, Gary?"

"Well, the lack of management witnesses to testify in my favor. None were called. Not one of my co-workers was called to testify regarding my performance. They told me they were willing to testify and they were not called."

"I see," Mark replied. "You know, General Motors would have retaliated against them too, if they had testified."

"Yeah, I know, but they are protected under Federal Laws if any retaliation occurred due to their testimony."

"I know that, Gary."

"The other basis for appeal, Mark, is the special verdict questions. The real issue between myself and General Motors was not resolved because of the inappropriate standard. My case is a civil trial, not a criminal one. I should not have to prove that General Motors' conduct was outrageous, reprehensible and egregious. That cannot be the standard of proof! Besides, the jury awarded me approximately $80,000, aside from the punitive damage issue. And somehow, Mark, you failed to collect that amount! The jury established liability against General Motors to the extent of the compensatory damage award, and we cannot collect it due to a technicality. Quite simply, a defect in the special verdict!"

"Well, Gary, I see," Mark stated.

"Wait a second, Mark. Hear me out. On the issue of punitive damages, I should be entitled. I don't understand how I cannot be given punitive damages after what you told me you filed in the original lawsuit."

"I see," Mark replied.

"Also, that one juror who called me after the trial indicated the jury had wanted to give $250,000 in compensatory damages and was persuaded not to by the car salesman. He's the very guy I told you not to put on the jury. Besides, other inappropriate comments and conduct occurred in the jury room. You need to look at all this, Mark. I don't quite understand why you haven't been successful in reaching a settlement with General Motors. What is going on here? I've worked substantially hard and made major contributions for General Motors, and before it came to all this I requested numerous transfers back to the New York/New Jersey area, only to be denied. General Motors has granted transfers and promotions for others. I know this is a very important and major operation for General Motors, however, I don't know why they wouldn't transfer me to a different facility. My appraisals, as you can see, were highly effective to outstanding. What the hell is happening here Mark?"

"What do you mean, Gary?"

"What I mean is, how can I work competently for General Motors, not be granted transfers from a hostile environment, not receive promotions or other entitlements, prove it before the Department of Labor, have the State Court jury establish liability of approximately $80,000 in compensatory damages, and not even be able to collect it? How can this be?"

"Well, Gary, that's the system," Mark said.

"System?! Mark, I know about systems. There are all kinds of systems. Some work and some don't. Maybe I should say many don't work. However, I do know they are capable of working, and we have to make this one work, too. This is why I hired you, Mark. This is your system. You went to school to learn about it, and there are procedures you must follow to make it work. This legal system we have here can work. What I am saying, Mark, is that what happened in that court room was not fair, and I do not agree with everything you did. I saw other obstacles too, and I am certain you saw them also."

"I know, Gary. Yes, I would have to agree with you. There were some obstacles, indeed."

"Mark, I know the people here do not like these issues. However, a deliberate wrong has been committed here and it has to stop. Besides, after looking at what occurred in the State Court, as measured by the results in this case, I would not be surprised if this would not be the foundation for a murder to be committed."

"Murder? What do you mean Gary?"

"Well, Mark, even though I told the jury nothing but the truth, it seemed as if someone did not want us to collect this little bit of money against General Motors. Although it was determined by the jury, due to a technicality in the special verdict, we cannot collect it. Therefore, even if General Motors had to pay this small sum to me, it was not enough to stop them from doing this to some other manager in the company. So what I mean about murder is that someone may try to kill another worker next time. After all, you remember the near-miss accident that occurred to me when Denis's brother, Chuck, almost hit me in the plant that morning I called your office. Eric Littrup walked by and turned his head while the truck was all over me. Did I deserve that?"

"No, Gary, you certainly did not," Mark replied.

"Mark, look into the appeal for me, okay?"

"Yeah, Gary. I will certainly look into the appeal and see what issues, if any, we can bring up."

"Do it right away. I mean soon, okay? After all, it's been a very long time already. Maybe you should try to settle this matter with a reasonable settlement, once and for all," I said.

"For what?"

"Oh, hell, I don't know . . . my job back or an alternative job. If they can't give me my old job back, with full restitution of all employment entitlements, in addition to $250,000 for the damages done to me or for $4.5 million if I don't continue my career with General Motors. I shouldn't have to explain to you how I arrived at that amount."

"Four and a half million dollars? Gary, you have to be kidding?"

"No, I'm not. I have permanent career damage as a result of General Motors' conduct and their attorney's assertions. This is what I think is reasonable, given what General Motors has done to me. This is nothing for a company its size. I was 28 when this happened to me and it could permanently hurt my career. You ought to know that, Mark."

"But, Gary, let's be reasonable."

"I am being reasonable. I'm willing to compromise. I'll tell you what. Get an economist to come up with the damage estimate or come back to me with General Motors' offer."

"What do you mean?" Mark asked.

"Leave it open for General Motors to come to me with a reasonable offer, or I will have no choice but to continue the litigation. Contact General Motors' attorneys and see if you can reach some kind of settlement. After all, you have the State Court issues for appeal and you have the wrongful discharge issue which we haven't yet litigated. However, in terms of what happened in State Court, I'd like you to bring up the issue in Federal Court. I thought that was where you were going to file the first lawsuit."

"Well, like I said before, it'll be more difficult for you to win in Federal Court. State Court would be better for you," Mark said.

"I know what you said, but the results didn't confirm it."

"In this situation, you're right. I don't know what happened."

"Well, some of it could have been politics. Maybe they didn't want us to win, and this is a message for others, regardless of your injuries."

"I don't think so, Gary," Mark said.

"I know, Mark; just speculating," I said. "Just see what you can do with General Motors and their attorneys."

A couple of weeks had gone by since my February meeting with Mark.

"Hon," my wife called, "you have a letter here from Mark."

"What does it say?"

"I didn't open it."

"Never mind. Give it to me. I'll read it."

"Well, Gary, what is it," she asked.

"Nothing to be concerned about. I'll get around it."

"What is it?" she asked.

"Mark said he is going to withdraw from the case unless I pay him the costs."

"Costs? Didn't you pay him?"

"I gave him a $1,500 retainer. I've paid him that, sure. He said it would cover some costs, but any costs above that would be paid after the case is over. The case isn't over yet because of the mistakes; there may be an appeal. Well, if he wants to withdraw, I'll have to let him. I can't pay him all the costs now because I may have to use this money to hire another lawyer to continue the litigation against General Motors."

"Another attorney?" my wife asked. "Don't you like Mark?"

"It isn't about like; it's not that at all. This is business, simply business. I guess I had a misunderstanding with him. Mark and I have some differences about this case . . . the witnesses, settlement, etc. Maybe I should let him withdraw. I don't want it to happen, but maybe it's best for the two of us and I'll just have to pay him later. My first priority is to keep this litigation going if General Motors doesn't want to settle. However, I will pay Mark if he did everything he should have. I can't run the risk of paying him and having him decide to withdraw anyway. The costs can't be that much. Even if I have to sell our home, which is worth more than $100,000, I could pay him that way."

"Sell our home? Gary, you don't want to do that," my wife said.

"No, you're right. I don't want to sell our home, and I shouldn't have to if the legal system works from a civil standpoint. However, it's the principle that's involved here. Mark knows I had to rebuild my income since my termination from General Motors and my income now is not that great. However, if these commission transactions come through, I'd recover.

"Well, I'm just going to have to get another attorney because I know Mark is going to withdraw. Quite frankly, I'm not going to stop him. If he wants to withdraw, then so be it."

For the next couple weeks, I interviewed, held meetings and conversed with several attorneys and law firms in the Milwaukee and Madison, Wisconsin areas.

"Fox, Fox, Schaefer, and Gingras," the receptionist answered. "May I help you?"

"Yes, is there an attorney Michael Fox there?" I asked.

"No, I'm sorry. He's not in."

"Well, is there an attorney Robert Gingras there?"

"Yes, there is," the receptionist responded.

"Can I talk to him?" I asked.

"Who's calling?"

"Gary McKnight," I replied.

"Hold on," the receptionist said.

"Bob Gingras."

"Mr. Gingras, this is Mr. McKnight speaking. I was referred to Michael Fox for an employment-related matter involving General Motors Corporation. I understand your firm handles these matters."

"Yes, we do. In fact, I am currently involved in a case against General Motors. I'm representing one of their female employees who was terminated," he said.

"I'm aware of that. However, I need to have a meeting with you or Mr. Fox regarding the essentials of my lawsuit against General Motors."

"Fine. Let me look at my schedule. How about next week?"

"Well, I need to meet with you as soon as possible. I'm pressed for time. My appeal has to be filed right away. I could quickly bring you up to date on the issues and facts of the case."

"Okay, how about this Thursday coming?"

"Fine, where are you located?" I said.

"44 East Mifflin Street, across from the State Capitol in Madison. Do you know where that is?"

"No, not exactly, but I'll find it. See you this Thursday, Mr. Gingras."

* * *

Since I knew I was scheduled to travel to Madison, Wisconsin in a few days, I thought it was necessary to provide a written chronology of the events and circumstances during my employment with General Motors, as well as the status of the legal bout with them.

It was already 1986 and this matter seemed to be just beginning. Keep in mind the complaint was filed with the Department of Labor in 1981 and then with the State Court in early 1983. There were numerous hurdles to overcome.

Apparently, General Motors representatives involved in my litigation quickly made the assessment that the issues involved were difficult to almost impossible for me to prove in court. In fact, I was told by a prominent Milwaukee attorney it would be a difficult case to win against General Motors because "there are so many variables you have to contend with in the process." Regardless, the many variables and hurdles I confronted had to be overcome. It is not my constitution to allow someone or some entity to deliberately wrong me without a meaningful response.

Chapter VII

Circumstantial Evidence and Murder

Finally, the week was coming to a close. It had been a rather unusual one. It seemed unusually long. One morning, my alarm went off at 4:30 a.m. Although I was normally fully alert, I felt very tired, as if I had not slept at all. First, I thought my tiredness was due to the commute to and from Chicago each week and often daily on the Amtrak train. Then I thought maybe I was coming down with the flu. I convinced myself, however, that it was more important for me to go to work than to stay home, even though it was the last day of the week.

I managed to pull myself out of bed and find my way to the shower. The cold water was refreshing, however, not enough to shake this feeling of tiredness. I then prepared a quick breakfast and felt much better.

As I opened the door to my home in search of the morning newspaper, the alarm on my clock went off again. I quickly closed the door and went back to shut off the alarm clock.

"Hon," my wife said, "what is that?"

"Oh, nothing. Just the alarm. It's okay now. Get some sleep," I responded.

During the time I had this brief conversation with my wife, I continued preparing for work. I threw on my shirt and suit. I had my tie in one hand and my briefcase in the other. I still had plenty of time to catch the morning Amtrak train which was scheduled to depart from downtown Milwaukee. It was 5:30 a.m. As I walked back to my bedroom to get my car keys, I heard a noise outside my door. I quickly went to my door and opened it to find no one there. I walked outside and looked around the area, but there was no one. Then I remembered to search for my newspaper again. I thought it strange it had not yet been delivered. I decided to get one later before I caught the train to Chicago, when I bought the Wall Street Journal.

"Hon, what time is it?" Shirley asked.

"It's 5:35 . . . time for me to go. I like to have enough time to park the car, listen to the morning news and review the results of the stock markets and other financial data."

"Aren't you going to kiss me good-bye?"

"Oh, sure. Hold on, dear. I have to get my other briefcase. The one I have here is not going to hold all the documents I have with me this morning. This one is much better. Now, let me (kiss) get out of here. The kids are still sleeping. Tell them I'll see them when I come home this evening. I'll call you before I get on the train. This way you can get some additional rest."

"That's really thoughtful of you, honey."

The car was parked down the street a short distance. When I tried to start it, it seemed dead. Looking under the hood, I found a loose battery cable and tightened it. I was glad it wasn't a more serious problem.

As soon as I got to the Amtrak station, I went to get the Wall Street Journal to read on the train before I got to the office. I purchased one and remembered I did not have the Milwaukee Sentinel. As I approached the vending machine for the Sentinel, I noticed it was sold out. Several more people had come afterward to purchase it only to be disappointed there were none left.

The train was boarding passengers but not leaving for a few minutes. I guessed I'd have time to buy a cup of coffee from the coffee shop, but it looked too crowded. I decided to wait until I got to Chicago. The long train ride from Milwaukee gave me time to research data and other financial information on companies I would recommend my clients invest in. Financial consultants and stockbrokers more or less have an insatiable appetite for any information which might have some relative impact in the financial markets. Their resources may include, but are not limited to, the Wall Street Journal, Financial Digest, Barron's, the New York Times, Forbes and a host of others, as well as local newspapers.

As I departed from the train, I looked around to see if I could purchase a copy of the Sentinel from a convenient vending machine. There were none in sight. I then walked to the newsstand to purchase one.

Shortly, following a brisk walk from the train station, I arrived at my office.

"Morning, Trisch. Hi, Anne. Any messages?"

"Yes, several. Here."

"Fine. Thank you."

"Hey, McKnight," I heard from further back in the office, "we have a meeting in the conference room. Are you coming?"

"Sure. I'll be there. I have to first get some information from the system and return several phone calls. I'll be there shortly. Hold a seat for me, will you?"

"Mr. McKnight, you have calls on lines one and two."

"Okay. Thank you, Diane." I picked up the phone and said, "Morning. Gary McKnight."

"Morning. How are things?"

"Fine, but I need you to return your option agreement form as soon as possible so we can get going with your particular investment program. I have a call waiting and I have to get into this meeting scheduled this morning. Don't forget to send those forms in. Thanks."

"Morning. McKnight."

"Hi, Mr. McKnight. You sent me some information on a security offering you're recommending."

"Why, yes. I thought it would be helpful to you in making a decision on what we were talking about as an appropriate investment for you. You still have time on this one. Let me get back to you later this morning. I have to go to a meeting now. I'll call you afterwards. Thanks. Bye."

"Mr. McKnight, you have calls on lines one and three."

"Diane, take messages on those calls. I have to go to a meeting now. Unless they're urgent, tell them I'll get back to them shortly."

No sooner did I enter the conference room of the Boutique Investment Firm and reach for a chair than I was told I had an important phone call.

"Let me get some coffee before I return. Hey, Mark, Dave, take some notes for me in the meeting. Nasser, give me those sheets in that offering. Morning everyone." Walking hurriedly from the conference back to my desk seemed an unusually long travel this morning, probably because I had to be in several places at the same time.

"Gary McKnight. How can I help . . . ?"

"McKnight? Listen."

"Who's this?"

"Listen, McKnight. I can't talk freely."

"Who is this? What . . . can't talk? What the . . . ?"

"Hey, man, did you hear about Littrup?" the caller said in a low voice.

"Littrup? You mean Eric Littrup? What about him?"

"Well . . . I mean . . . his son? Littrup's son . . . he killed this guy."

"He did what!? To who? Anybody I know?"

"They said . . . I mean it's all over the fucking newspaper . . . this morning's Sentinel."

"Wait a second. Hold on. Where is Eric?"

"I don't know. They said he was in a daze. They couldn't talk to him. They said . . . ."

"Hold on! Who the fuck is 'they' ?"

"Shop talk has it that Eric Littrup appeared to be dazed and distraught when he found out his son's involvement in the murder hit the newspaper and was talked about throughout the plant."

"Eric's son . . . murder? I can't believe what's happening here!"

"Hey, McKnight, didn't you see it in the morning Sentinel?"

"No. For some reason I couldn't get my hands on one this morning. I couldn't find one anywhere. Not even on the train . . . ."

"The Milwaukee Sentinel reported that Kirk Littrup, Eric's son, conspired with his co-worker, Pickett, to murder their supervisor."

"What!?"

"The Milwaukee Sentinel further revealed the two had planned the murder before and decided to murder their supervisor on a third shift operation. The two had talked about getting rid of their supervisor, Waricak, by getting him fired or killing him and disposing of the body."

"How could they do that? Did the article mention if he was drugged?"

"Drugged? What do you mean?"

"Did they drug him first? What happened?"

"The article said they hit him several times on the back of the head with a crowbar and continued striking him as he fell to the floor. They tied him up with rope and stuffed him in a 55-gallon drum."

"This is deep. Look, I have to go, I have to get some work out."

"Hold on. The rumor has it that General Motors is planning on promoting Eric and transferring him to a different plant."

"Promoting him? Transferring him? Well, I guess he was going to get the promotion, anyway. Look, I have to confirm what you're saying. This is a tragedy; indeed, it is. Before I go, how did they get caught?"

"Well, from what I can gather from the newspaper and the shop talk, a garbage truck driver began compacting the barrel's contents and saw a hand. That's how they discovered it."

"I just don't understand this. I did my work at General Motors and Eric got rid of me. My appraisal in manufacturing was highly effective. And now, Eric's son decides to get rid of someone permanently. Is this for real? Hey, I've got to go."

"Okay, man. See ya."

I continued my work and throughout the day received a couple additional calls confirming what the first caller had said. I began thinking about my experiences at the General Motors facility involving a near-miss accident and a request by one of the defendants to have me work on a third shift operation at the GM facility.

Later I made a couple phone calls, including one to attorney Bob Gingras. That evening, I thought about the occurrence off and on during my train ride from home.

And they say these things don't happen. I worked for the best interest of the company and look what happened?

Although I discussed this with my wife, I did not discuss it with anyone outside the General Motors environment other than Bob Gingras and a close associate. Maybe only an etiologist or forensic expert could determine the cause or connection and the meaning of this. This was a rather mysterious development and an intriguing phenomenon to surface during my involvement with the General Motors Corporation case.

CHAPTER VIII

Federal District Court Trial

"Now you see, Bob. The first day of trial didn't go that badly, did it?"

"Gary, it's only the beginning," Bob said. "Can you meet this evening at the Holiday Inn? I need to discuss more information with you regarding this case."

"I can meet you at 6:30 tonight. I just have to make some arrangements to have my kids taken care of. My wife works for the government and she's in training this week in Chicago. Fine time for her to be called away for training . . . the same week I am scheduled for a major trial."

"Well, as I said before, I think you're making a mistake by going to trial. You're going to lose. We should not be taking this matter to court. General Motors' witnesses are going to hurt you."

"Let's just talk about it later tonight, Bob."

"Do you want to meet at the Holiday Inn, off College? That's where I'm staying," said Bob.

"Fine. I'll meet you in the dining room at 6:30 p.m. That ought to give me enough time to get them settled in."

Later that evening at the Holiday Inn the waitress asked, "Can I help you, sir?"

"Yes. I am looking for a Bob Gingras. Oh, there he is. Hi, Bob."

"Hi, Gary. Look, I've been thinking. You're wrong for taking this matter to trial; you're going to lose."

"Listen, Bob! I don't want to lose my professionalism here! I am pretty damn upset right now and I don't need you to cause me to increase my frustrations."

"Yeah, I know, Gary, but their witnesses can hurt you."

"Bob! Damn it! Listen to me! I don't care about their witnesses! You've had the evidence in this case for a long time now! Besides, I'm telling the truth and you have the evidence to prove it! If you balance everything and locate my witnesses . . . . you haven't even talked to them yet . . . you would understand why I think this case is winnable. All I want you to do is to stay focused on the issues of this case and practice law."

"Gary, you're wrong."

"Bob, I don't care if I am wrong. My reputation and career have been substantially injured and it hurts my family, my friends. Don't you understand!? Don't get me wrong. I'm not a difficult person. I am trying very hard not to be difficult with you, but you are giving me the impression that you don't understand what's at stake here! I know you lost your case in State Court and Federal Court with my colleague, Virnesse, but this is a different case entirely. I will point out to you the facts and issues and help you with the witnesses. All I want you to do is to stay focused. Practice law! It's just that simple. Stop fighting with me!

"Right now, the position you have me in is fighting you and General Motors and their lawyers. Why didn't you tell me how you felt about your position sooner? It's too late for you to tell me what you think now. I have been hurt badly on Wall Street financially because of adverse market conditions. The firms did not close the multi-million dollar transactions I brought them. Besides, this case has spilled over to my employer. As you know, I was threatened with termination . . . even there."

"Yeah, I know about your earnings. You've made more money working on Wall Street than at General Motors in some respects, but in most respects you haven't."

"Well, it depends on how you look at it. As I explained to you before, because of this involvement, my earnings and career have not yet stabilized. For several years, my earnings have been substantially lower than my earnings while working at General Motors. However, there may be something going on here regarding my earnings with the investment firm," I said.

"What do you mean, Gary?"

"Bob, I've gone over this with you before. I've brought in several large, multi-million dollar investment transactions and developed domestic and international corporate relationships, including Japan and other significant accounts. You have all this information. I've sent you several documents and summaries as well as significant factual information for the General Motors lawsuit. I've also sent you several letters discussing what occurred to me, since on several occasions you were simply not available. Bob, maybe you had your mind set on settling my lawsuit with General Motors for $3000 or $3500, but this is absolutely ridiculous. I can't believe you."

"Gary, I said maybe I could get you $10,000 or $15,000, and that $3,000 is what General Motors is offering. I strongly encouraged you to take it."

"Bob, my fucking life and reputation have been substantially damaged by General Motors' representatives, their lawyers and whoever else is involved here. I've done my job very well at General Motors, as you know. Before suing General Motors my performance ratings were highly effective to outstanding with the potential to attain unclassified levels, the levels attained by the people who run General Motors."

"Gary, you're wrong."

"Bob, why are you doing this to yourself? Why are you taking this grief from me when you should stay focused on the facts and issues of this case?"

"Gary, I'm well aware of the facts and issues of your case, and I recommend you settle it here."

"Just who are you representing, Bob? Me or General Motors?"

"You, of course, Gary."

"Like hell you are, Bob. You want me to settle this case for $3000 when my whole life is in disarray as a result of this litigation. My rights have been violated, as have the rights of my friends and the people around me. This is clearly and simply a violation of the law. What the fuck can I do with $3000? The legal costs of this litigation far exceed that amount, and you are talking about my career, my career! I do want my position back, assignments I should be entitled to, or some other arrangement if I can't get my job back. This has a value far above any $3000 or $3500 you're suggesting I take."

"Gary, you have to understand you're in front of a difficult and unpredictable judge."

"Who's the judge again?"

"Judge Gordon. He's unpredictable."

"Then that means I do have some chance of winning."

"No, Gary. It's too difficult."

"Bob, time out! Enough is enough! Let's get focussed here for the second day of trial. Just because I disagree with you doesn't mean I want you working against me. I don't need this."

Bob shook his head from side to side with deep frustration. "Gary, would you like some coffee?" he asked.

"No, I don't want any coffee," I said. "Let's just get on with the trial and my witnesses and see how they may be able to help you."

*   *   *

Following the McKnight v. General Motors trial at the Federal District level in the Eastern District of Wisconsin, Robert Gingras and I prepared to go at it once again in the State Circuit Court in Milwaukee County with other claims involving General Motors under the statute.

It appeared as if Gingras and I had a cooperative relationship at the time I hired him in May of 1986. At that time, it seemed as if he was complying with my instructions, although I wanted other issues addressed as well. My primary interest was to resolve the wrongs perpetrated against me by General Motors. I also wanted to collect the State Court jury award and other damages. Eventually, we had some disagreements, but nothing I thought we couldn't overcome.

"Well, Bob, since you've rejected several of my previous settlement demands, just to close this matter I'm willing to accept $450,000. Besides, I am tired of debating with you on these matters. I want to focus on my career and move ahead."

"Gary, $450,000 is a ridiculous offer. General Motors knows the case is worth far less than that. You're wasting your time if you think you can get that kind of recovery."

"Bob, maybe I'm wrong on the settlement amount, but I don't think so. I think this case is worth considerably more, but I'm tired of arguing with you with regard to what I think. This is why I hired you in the first place. Isn't it?"

"You wanted me to handle the State Court appeal and the wrongful termination, and you asked me to look into some other legal issues."

"That's partly correct. But I hired you to do the things you've said as well as use good judgment in resolving the issues. I hired you to think, Bob! I know you're a capable attorney!"

"That I've done, Gary."

"As far as you're concerned, Bob, but not as far as I am. I'm not satisfied with what you're recommending. It doesn't make sense. I've told you the facts of my case and General Motors' motives for terminating me. It was not proper. I completed all my assignments, and my work performance was no different than anyone else's. I was treated differently, harassed and wrongfully terminated as the evidence shows. This treatment is injurious to my career."

"Gary, I hear what you're saying. In no way will General Motors and their attorneys settle this case for what you're asking."

"General Motors has the State Circuit Court case on appeal to think about and that does not even include the other case."

"Well, after evaluating your chances of winning the appeal, I don't think you have a chance there. I am telling you to come up with a reasonable offer so I can see if General Motors will accept it."

"Bob, if you'd listen to me, we could win this thing. I've been wrongfully terminated. There was nothing wrong with my performance!"

"What is your demand? And not what you've indicated before."

"We're going to win the appeal and we're going to win the other trial. If you're not with me here, then settle the damn thing. Why are you so quick to give up? Can't you negotiate further on this? What does your partner think about this?"

"He'll agree on what I decide."

"Have you talked to him about this?"

"Yes. He's going to agree with what I recommend."

"You're making a serious mistake here, Bob. It's just my gut reaction. This case has tremendous value if you work it right."

"Gary, what is your demand? Come on, I need it now."

"Oh, hell, $95,000."

"Gary, General Motors is not going to settle then."

"So? That's why you're a lawyer. Get more. Then let the jury decide. The case is worth more, and a jury will see that. The Circuit Court case on appeal is at least worth that."

"No, it isn't, Gary."

"Yes, Bob. The jury assessed damages of $80,000 and there were too many problems with the jury, the jury instructions and the standard of proof for me to prevail. Settle it for $90,000. That's it. I'm done. Get back to me, Bob. I'm tired of debating with you. Ninety thousand, that's it. You're talking my job, my career."

"Okay."

Several weeks passed before Bob sent me a letter indicating my settlement demand was such that General Motors' defense attorneys would not counter offer. In fact, he stated I was unreasonable.

I acknowledged General Motors' position and encouraged Bob to stay focused on the issues and continue development of the case for trial. Shortly afterward, the Circuit Court trial on appeal would come down from the Wisconsin Appellate Court. I was successful. The Appellate Court remanded my Circuit Court case and requested a new trial.

The Circuit Court trial was scheduled for August of 1989. The Federal Court trial was held in October of 1988. I prevailed in my trial in Federal Court against General Motors.

"Hi, Honey," my wife said as I returned home. "What would you like for dinner?"

"Whatever you decide. Hey, why don't we go out for dinner?"

"That sounds like a good idea."

"How about the Hilton or the Hyatt downtown, or Maders, wherever?"

"This time of night? Gary, I'll have to get dressed. I have nothing prepared to go there."

"Let's take the kids with us."

"Then let's go to Red Lobster or Chi Chi's."

"Sure. Okay. Get the kids."

"Can we afford this, dear?"

"No, not really. We'll work it in anyway. Don't worry."

"You've been managing closely by the vest for several years."

"I know, most people do when they lose their job. It's certainly not easy starting over again."

"When are you going to get your job back? You won your case several months ago."

"I don't know. Bob said Judge Gordon was not going to give me my job back because General Motors was hostile."

"So what are you going to do?"

"Well, I had Bob ask for my previous job back and if the judge denies me that, I'll see if he'll consider putting me in an alternative position, another management position or a position in corporate finance, tax or investment banking . . . whatever we can identify as an alternative. I asked Bob to handle this carefully. I don't know all the positions that exist within General Motors. Let's go."

At that moment the phone rang. "Hello?"

"Hi, Gary. How are you, son?"

"Okay, Ma. How about yourself?"

"Okay, I guess. I'm still here, thanks to the Lord."

"How's the family and the kids?"

"Fine, they're okay. Could be better you know."

"I would like to see everybody."

"You're welcome to come out here anytime you like, but we'll probably come out there this summer for a week or so."

"Good. I'd love to see everybody."

"Same here. How's everybody out there?"

"Okay. People are always asking about you."

"Well, that's good. Tell them I said hello. I'll talk to you another time, Mother. I was just about to take the kids and Shirley out to dinner."

"Oh, that's nice. Okay, Gary. I'll talk to you later. Bye, love you."

"Love you too, Ma!"

"Gary, come on. The kids are in the car waiting. Let's go."

"I'll be right there, Hon."

The phone rang again. "Hello?"

"McKnight, how are you doing?"

"Okay. Wilbert is this you?"

"Yeah, what are you doing?"

"I was just on my way out to take my wife and kids to get something to eat."

"Oh, well, I'll let you go."

"Gary, come on. What's taking you so long?" Shirley asked.

"Wilbert, I have to go now. I'll call you back."

"Hon, what are you doing?"

"Oh, that was Wilbert on the phone just now. I told him I'd get back to him because we were going out."

"Let's go before it gets too late."

CHAPTER IX

Matter of Controversy

It was a beautiful day in July of 1990. I drove down Lincoln Memorial Drive past Lake Michigan and its white, sandy beach filled with beach-goers who were engaged in various activities. The drive was slower than usual since several beach-goers were taking their time crossing the heavily traveled road from their parking and picnic areas across from the beach. These were the unfortunate ones who were unable to secure a picnic area or parking on the beach side.

As I continued to drive south on Lincoln Memorial Drive, I decided to park my car and walk across to the beach to absorb the enjoyment of a more natural and mundane way of life. I was not properly attired to be there. I had just left the business establishment of a friend and had on my suit and tie. I had to wait several minutes before I could leave my car and go across to the beach. There were a lot of cars traveling along the drive that day. I decided since it was around the lunch hour I could take a few moments to enjoy this marvelous occasion. I removed my jacket, took off my tie, socks and shoes, rolled up the sleeves of my thin white shirt and proceeded to the beach.

As I continued to the beach, it seemed as if everyone was enjoying himself in whatever he was doing—playing volleyball, building sand castles, reading, swimming or playing football. Several people were sun bathing and others were playing with frisbees. It seemed as if no one there was concerned with anything other than enjoying this beautiful day.

Along the coastlines of the lake several groups of people were participating in water activities from water-skiing and sailing to speedboat racing. Standing there, I could hear the thrashing sounds of the waves as they splashed unrelentlessly against the shoreline. The sun was bright and hot and underneath it all was a continuous, cool lake breeze which seemed to travel with each wave as it made its way to the shore. At times the waves approached the shoreline, which was protected by glacier-like white rocks, and climbed the height of the huge rocks.

This was just a prelude to an outstandingly gorgeous day. I felt compelled to spend more time here, however, I had to get on with other requirements of the day. I got into my car, redressed and proceeded along Lincoln Memorial Drive to the expressway, traveling southwest. I stopped home before going back to the office. I wanted to check for messages on my answering machine, take a shower and change clothes.

The beautiful thoughts of the beach visit were still with me as I showered. The lukewarm water was rejuvenating as it cleansed my skin. When I stepped out of the shower, the phone rang. It was my wife.

"Hi, Hon . . . okay. I stopped home to take a shower and change clothes. I'm going back to the office later. Okay . . . sure . . . okay. Hey, I have to go now. I have to finish dressing. I will call you later. Sure. Bye."

No sooner had I finished buttoning the last button at my neckline before securing my tie, than the phone rang again. I decided to let it ring a second and third time.

"Hello?" For a moment it seemed as if no one was there. "Hello, hello?" There was such a delay of caller response that I started to hang up.

Suddenly I heard, "Gary," very softly, then "Gary, Gary," again very softly.

"Yeah?"

"This is Bob Gingras. How are you?"

"Fine, Bob. It's a beautiful day." Bob did not respond. There was a silence on the phone. "Bob, did you hear me?"

"Yeah, Gary, I heard you."

"What are you calling about, Bob?" He still did not respond quickly. "I'm calling about the appeal in your General Motors matter. What are you doing tomorrow, Gary?"

"I'm not certain. I haven't talked to my wife about her plans. Why? Is there something wrong?"

"I'm wondering if you can come to Madison tomorrow, to my office."

"Can't we talk about this over the telephone?"

"No, Gary. I think you should come up to my office to talk with me about the appeal."

"Did we get an unfavorable decision on appeal, Bob?" There was no immediate response. "Bob? Bob? Can you hear me?"

"Yeah, Gary. Yes. I mean, yes and no."

"To what extent was it unfavorable?"

"Gary, let's not go into it here and now. I want to talk with you in my office regarding the decision."

"I know you don't want to discuss this matter now, but there are things I must know. Did we lose everything?"

"No, Gary."

"Bob, what is going on? Answer me! Did we lose?"

"I said, no, Gary. Please, let's talk about it tomorrow."

"Tomorrow! Let's talk now, Bob! Did you hold on to any of the cash judgment?"

"Gary, we can talk about it when I see you."

"Bob, I need to know. My house could be in jeopardy if you do not recover the punitive damage and compensatory damage awards. As you know, I had to borrow $70,000 against my home since I was not paid the judgment at the time of trial, or reinstated by the judge. You told me it would take no more than six months to collect."

"I know."

"Then what's going on? Tell me."

"I don't know. It was a bad decision."

"A bad decision? I don't understand."

"Well, Gary, you see, the panel decided against you regarding your claims, due to other court rulings."

"What rulings, Bob?"

"Well, it was the Patterson ruling. I don't want to talk about it now."

"Tell me now, exactly what was affected? Tell me at least some of it so I can be prepared for tomorrow."

"Now is not good at all. I just got the information myself."

"Talk to me, Bob. Let me know something."

"Well, Gary, I'm not entirely certain about all the particulars of the Seventh Circuit decision. I know they reversed part of the judgment and remanded back to the District Court other aspects of the case."

"Reversed?!"

"Gary, let's not talk now. I'm not prepared to discuss this matter."

"Bob, what was reversed?"

"They reversed the issue of punitive damages under Patterson."

"Wait a second. They did what?"

"Gary, listen to me. I know it's not good. Can you meet me tomorrow?"

"I don't know. Let me look at my schedule. Sure. I'll meet you in your office first thing tomorrow. I don't believe this. How can you lose that much money?" I said.

"I know, Gary. It's hard for me to believe."

"I don't know how the Seventh Circuit Court of Appeals would allow General Motors and their attorneys to benefit from the Patterson decision. They never talked about Patterson before. How can this happen? You've got to be kidding. I guess we go to the U.S. Supreme Court from here."

"Well, that's something for us to consider. Can you come to Madison tomorrow?"

"Yeah. I'll be at your office first thing tomorrow. Do you realize you just interrupted a perfect day?"

"Yeah, Gary. Mine too."

I slammed the phone down nearly breaking the receiver. I snatched it up again and slammed the entire unit up against the wall, pushing aside several briefs which were on my nearby dining room table.

"I can't believe it! How could Bob allow the Seventh Circuit to set aside $750,000 in punitive damages and interest? How the hell can this be allowed?"

The phone rang again. It was Wilbert. "I tried to call you a few minutes ago. Were you on the phone?"

"Yeah, but I'm getting ready to get out of here now," I said.

"What's happening with your appeal? Haven't you heard anything?"

"Well, I have to talk with Bob later about the status of the appeal. I'm meeting with him tomorrow to find out exactly what's happening with it. Wilbert, call me later. Now is not a good time to talk about this. I have to go now. Call me next week, on Monday. Let me get out of here before something else happens."

The phone rang again. It was my wife. "You're still there?" she asked.

"Yes. What do you think? I did answer the phone, you know."

"I thought you were preparing to leave some time ago."

"I was, and I am leaving now."

"Why didn't you leave sooner?"

"Well, Bob called and he wants me to come to Madison tomorrow to discuss the Appeals Court decision."

"What about the decision? What happened?"

"According to Bob, we were reversed on the punitive damage issue because of the U.S. Supreme Court ruling in Patterson. I want to make certain that's the only reason we were reversed, and that it's not due to some legal technicality."

"I know," Shirley replied. "When will you know, tomorrow?"

"Not necessarily. You know Bob's not going to tell me everything. His meetings may allow him enough time to talk about everything, but certainly not all the particulars of the decision. He seemed as if he did not want to talk about everything. Shirley, I don't want to discuss this now."

"I know, Gary, but did the Appeals Court reverse all our money?"

"No, not all of it, but most of it, as I understand from Bob."

"I don't quite understand."

"I know. No one seems to understand, as you can gather from the tone of my voice. Look, Shirley, I will talk with you later. I have to go now."

Everything seemed to have been going well until Bob notified me of the Seventh Circuit Court of Appeals decision. After having several conversations throughout the day with various people, the rest of the day appeared to have a huge cloud over it.

In the
United States Court of Appeals
For the Seventh Circuit

Nos. 89-1379, 89-1526
Gary McKnight,
Plaintiff-Appellee, Cross-Appellant,

v.

General Motors Corporation,
Defendant-Appellant, Cross-Appellee.

Appeal from the United States District Court
for the Eastern District of Wisconsin.
No. 87 C 0248—Myron L. Gordon, Judge.

Argued February 12, 1990—Decided July 2, 1990

Before Posner and Easterbrook, Circuit Judges, and Fairchild, Senior Circuit Judge.

Posner, Circuit Judge. Gary McKnight brought suit under 42 U.S.C. sec. 1981 (which dates back to the Civil Rights Act of 1866,) and Title VII of the Civil Rights Act of 1964, 42 U.S.C. sec. 2000e, claiming that General Motors fired him both because he is black and also in retaliation for his having filed claims of racial discrimination against the company. A jury returned a verdict for McKnight on the section 1981 claim, awarding him $110,000 in compensatory damages (of which half represented back pay) and $500,000 in punitive damages. On the basis of the jury's verdict, the judge entered judgment for McKnight in the Title VII count as well but declined to order him reinstated—the only relief, besides back pay, that McKnight had requested under Title VII. General Motors appeals from the judgment against it and McKnight cross-appeals from the denial of reinstatement.

While this case was before us, the Supreme Court decided Patterson v. McLean Credit Union, 109 S. Ct. 2363 (1989), and we must decide whether, as urged by General Motors, Patterson wipes out McKnight's section 1981 claims. General Motors did not question the applicability of section 1981 to McKnight's claims in the district court, and the failure to urge a point in the trial court ordinarily forfeits the right to urge it on appeal. Yet the principle that judicial decisions normally are applied retroactively, and so to cases pending on appeal when the decision was made, EEOC v. Vucitech, 842 F.2d 936, 941 (7th Cir. 1988), was held in Carroll v. General Accident Ins. Co., 891 F.2d 1174, 1175 n. 1 (5th Cir. 1990), to require the application of Patterson to a case—a discharge case like this—pending on appeal even though the defendant had failed to question the applicability of section 1981 in the district court. Is this holding sound?

Patterson was a racial-harassment case rather than a discharge case, and the Supreme Court affirmed the court of appeals, which had held that racial harassment was not actionable under section 1981. It was only after oral argument that the Supreme Court, in an order setting the case for reargument, 108 S. Ct. 1419 (1988) (per curiam), requested the parties to brief the question whether Runyon v. McCrary, 429 U.S. 160 (1976), which had held that section 1981 forbids private as well as public discrimination, and which the court of appeals in Patterson had not even cited, should be overruled. In the end, the Court decided not to overrule Runyon, but in the course of its wide-ranging reexamination of section 1981 indicated (as it seems to us) that claims of racially motivated discharge are not actionable under that statute. This result could not reasonably have been anticipated before the order setting the case for reargument. ("Claims of racially discriminatory . . . firing . . . fall easily within sec. 1981's protection." Patterson v. McLean Credit Union, 805 F.2d 1143, 1145 (4th Cir. 1986), aff'd, 109 S. Ct. 2363 (1989).) A party should be allowed to take advantage of a decision rendered during the pendency of his case, even if he had not reserved the point decided, if the decision could not reasonably have been anticipated. A contrary rule would induce parties to drown the trial judge with reservations.

But the order to reargue Patterson was issued more than five months before the trial in the present case began. General Motors had plenty of time in which to mount a timely challenge to applicability of section 1981, and we may assume that by doing so it would have preserved its right to rely on the peculiar and unexpected course that Patterson in the end took; that was to overrule Runyon with respect to some discriminatory conduct but not other, although the conduct no longer actionable includes, as we shall see, the type of discriminatory conduct charged in this case. But General Motors did not question the applicability of section 1981 to this case until Patterson was decided, by which time the trial was over and the case was in this court.

Even if by this delay General Motors waived its right to invoke Patterson, a question we need not answer, McKnight cannot benefit. For while vigorously contesting the applicability of Patterson to the facts of his case, he has never argued that General Motors has waived its right to rely on Patterson. A defense of waiver is itself waivable. McKnight waived any defense of waiver that he may have had. United States v. Rodriguez, 888 F.2d 519, 524 (7th Cir. 1989).

McKnight makes two claims under section 1981, and we must now consider the impact of the Patterson decision on each. The claims are termination on grounds of race and retaliation for filing antidiscrimination complaints.

[Mr. McKnight is a member of the black race. Cases involving matters of race or creed are litigated under the same statute as the McKnight case, as well as cases of women who are precluded or have issues involving sexual discrimination or harassment claims.]

*   *   *

We had just come off a long, harsh, cold winter. During this time of year, the effects of winter had dissipated. It was now April of 1991.

"Hon," I called to my wife, "I'm going to the Greendale Courts to shoot some ball."

"Who are you going with?" she asked.

"Myself. All my boys are out east, with the exception of a few here in Milwaukee. If Kim were here, I would take her with me so she could play tennis while I work out on the court."

"Well, why don't you wait for her? She'll be back soon."

"She's outside playing with Bridget and Melany," I said. "Besides, there's always someone on the court to run a game of ball with. It's not the same as running a game of ball with the guys you grew up with, though. You know what I mean?"

"Yeah, I know," she said.

"Before I go, did the mail come yet? I'm expecting some important mail from Bob's office regarding a hearing on several important issues as to the General Motors litigation."

"I haven't seen the mailman, But what hearing's this?" Shirley asked.

"Well, I don't want to go into this now; however, it's a special hearing before Judge Gordon on matters of reinstatement to a position with General Motors or some alternative value for my job at General Motors if I am not reinstated."

"Judge Gordon? Reinstatement? Alternative value? What are you talking about? I thought the U.S. Supreme Court did not hear your case."

"That's correct. The U.S. Supreme Court did not grant me certiorari (cert). They decided not to hear my case vis a vis the Patterson decision which adversely affected my case to begin with."

"Well, then, what are you talking about?" Shirley asked.

"You see, the issue of my case before the U.S. Supreme Court related to their ruling in the Patterson decision. This decision primarily pertains to the `damage' question in my case and not at all to the issues of my case."

"Well, if the Supreme Court does not hear your case, isn't it over?"

"No, not at all," I said. "The 'damage' issues under section 1981 were affected by the Patterson decision in 1990 before the U.S. Court of Appeals for the Seventh Circuit Title VII were affected. Title VII is substantially inequitable in this conservative climate. This is why I was argumentative with Bob Gingras regarding the issue of reinstatement and alternative value as the prevailing party against General Motors. This is why I told him to appeal those issues before the Seventh Circuit. It was my gut feeling General Motors and their legal representatives and, perhaps, many others, did not want to see me get the original judgement the jury gave me, which was a lot. Besides, you know the problems I had with Bob Gingras, fighting with him to litigate this case. I don't like that. The courts are extremely conservative. If Bob had been able to hold onto my original judgment it would have been well over $1,000,000 by now. Instead, he made a huge mistake by not filing the waiver according to the U.S. Court of Appeals for the Seventh Circuit. Now we're losing our home simply because of the mistakes and delays of the case, and the fact that I have not been paid yet.

"That much? A million dollars?!" she said.

"Yeah. Why do you think I'm so firm with Bob? After all, I was the one who was substantially injured, as well as my family. I simply do not understand Bob at all. I've had to fight and argue with him on several different issues as if I were fighting General Motors. Even now, the case wouldn't have survived if I didn't assert myself with him and demand he cross appeal these issues. I would quite simply be out of contention with General Motors. This case would have been closed a long time ago. Bob Gingras wants me to have what he wants me to have, and it seems it's not what the Law or Congress allows."

"You mean the case would be over?"

"Yes, that's right. I would not have been able to continue this litigation. The only issue to be resolved would be my lost wages from my time off the job. That is substantially lower than what I should actually be entitled to receive. This is why I am so fucking frustrated. This really makes me angry."

"Gary, calm down," Shirley said.

"Why do I have to pull teeth with Bob? What the fuck is going on with this guy anyway? Something is not fucking right. Someone is not on the level here. I have been substantially injured with permanent career damages. I haven't been too hard on Bob Gingras, and he keeps trying to sell me a bag of shit."

"Gary, hold on. Calm down."

"I simply can't believe this. I won my case against General Motors before a Federal Jury. We're losing our home, and Bob doesn't seem to be representing all my interests. I just don't understand Bob. Why is he so fucking containing? The Federal, Congressional and U.S. Supreme Courts say I am entitled to certain remedies for winning my case, and that's what I want! Nothing more . . . nothing less! What Bob wants me to have is fucking ridiculous. If I accept, he'll be making me a loser. I don't need my fucking lawyer to cause me to be worse off financially after winning against General Motors!

"Bob keeps telling me its the judges who are causing the problems for us now. Keep in mind that it was Bob Gingras who argued with me in his office and told me I was completely wrong to take this matter to trial because I would lose. Bob . . . not the judges! It was Bob Gingras who argued with me to settle this case for $3000 to $3500 against General Motors because I was going to lose . . . not the judges. It was Bob Gingras who told me I was not entitled to reinstatement or front pay as alternative compensation . . . not the judges. The fucking statute provides for these things. I've read them myself. I don't understand what the fuck Bob is trying to do to us! I've not done anything to this guy! Why doesn't he want to see us get this judgement and all these entitlements? Is it his ego? Can't he accept some advice from his damn client for a change!? Look, I have to go, Hon. I am sorry."

"Okay." (kiss)

It was a beautiful day. One could see almost a complete transformation of the season. The trees and the grass were bearing their bright green colors of spring, and there was a brisk, cool breeze of mountain-like freshness. The sun's rays complemented the beautiful surroundings of the landscape. The basketball court was surrounded by large, beautiful trees and a well-manicured lawn. The brisk breeze whisked through the area muffling the sounds of children's chatter at a nearby playground. The basketball court was fresh with new rims, A-1 nets and players anxiously waiting for a game to start. Time indeed had gone bye. Although I saw several spectators my age and older, the players ranged from ages 18 to 34.

As I made my entrance into the gate of the court, I was immediately summoned to play ball. Sides of five were chosen, and we introduced ourselves. A full court game commenced very quickly and lasted for an hour and fifteen minutes or so of fast-paced, unrefereed basketball. At the completion of the first game, a second game began without hesitation and lasted as long as the first.

As I looked across to the baseball field, I could see a game just beginning, and the tennis players on the court were actively engaged in serious play.

We began a third game after rotating players and adding some new ones who had come on the court. The basketball court was full with several spectators, far different than what I was accustomed to back East in the city. It was different . . . much different. Without your buddies, those you grew up with, it's not the same. However unfortunate it may seem, this is partly what life is all about, anyway. As I was leaving the court, everyone banded together in groups and showed they were completely content being as they were all from the same neighborhood. Again I found myself on someone else's turf, as with everything else I was involved in during my residency in the State of Wisconsin. I was always on someone's turf, an outsider. Although I am a U.S. born American citizen, I felt like I was in a different country.

I felt my career had been substantially damaged and contained here. It seemed as if Wisconsin were a very restrictive environment compared to the New York area. Here, I was always tested and singled out for some unknown reason, although I possessed a high level of motivation to accomplish a lot and to be actively involved in many different things. Why would someone do something to slow me down by containing my aspirations, motivations, career endeavors or anything I was involved in? It began to appear as if I were not getting any help or support from anyone. I simply could not understand Wisconsinites with their conservative values.

The legal involvement against General Motors Corporation only complicated matters. What did they want with me? Does anyone really know? I didn't mind litigating issues I believed in, but I simply couldn't fight with those who are supposed to know the law. General Motors has hundreds and hundreds of lawyers representing them, not including their legal staff within the corporation. They have many investigators and hundreds of auditors outside: Deloitt Haskins, Sells and Bankers, Morgan, Standly, several politicians and many, many others. General Motors even gave John Delorean a run for his money, eventually resulting in charges of criminal prosecution for the one time GM executive.

Even in my case, I had not received a dime from General Motors since 1983, and my case was still pending with a host of legal issues to be resolved. I had a lawyer with whom I had to fight on entitlement issues. Why was I being contained, as this involvement was an image thing, as if someone thought I wanted to be Governor or Vice President of the United States at some point? I was not treated this way when I lived on the East Coast.

It seemed as if the people here were wasting my time and deliberately wasting my life. I began to question my attorney's business capacity as a decision maker and his aptitude to understand all my concerns. The issues Bob was to resolve were normal business to be taken care of legally by him and pursued in a professional manner before the courts. I expected all my entitlements as proscribed by the Law and the U.S. Constitution, but I lost so much as a result of this involvement with the mistakes and delays.

As I continued my drive, I decided to take the scenic route through the tree-lined entrance of Whitnall Park, complemented by its carefully manicured grass of a deep green color and mansion-like homes in the background. As soon as I arrived home, I greeted my wife.

"Hi, Hon. Did the mail come?"

"Yeah. It's on the table."

"Here's something from Gingras. I have to go to Madison next week to meet with him at his office."

*　　*　　*

In June of 1989, the U.S. Supreme Court provided its decision regarding the meaning of Section 1981 of the Civil Rights Bill and the Patterson case before it. The Supreme Court decided Section 1981 of the Civil Rights Bill concerned conduct during the initial formation of making a contract. More specifically, the statute concerned itself with conduct during the initial hire. The Supreme Court further stated that remedies not available under Section 1981 for injured parties would generally be available under Title VII of the Civil Rights Bill of 1964 which was signed into law by President Lyndon B. Johnson. However, since the more severe injuries occurred to individuals after the initial hire and at some other point during the course of employment, compensatory and punitive damages would not be available to those so injured. In general, punitive and compensatory damages are the bulk of such a litigant's award.

The case of McKnight v. General Motors was pending during the U.S. Supreme Court's deliberations regarding the meaning of Section 1981 as it related to Patterson v. McClean Credit Union.

In fact, my case, McKnight v. General Motors had already been fully tried in the Federal District Court for the Eastern District in Wisconsin. I won my case before the Federal District Court as decided by a federal jury in October of 1988. The case had been instructed under the Civil Rights Statute of 1866, more specifically Section 1981 and Title VII of the Civil Rights Bill of 1964. The Federal jury awarded me $55,000 in back pay, $55,000 in compensatory damages and $500,000 in punitive damages. There were other entitlements as well, such as reinstatement and attorney fees and costs. I had a lot to lose if my case on appeal was not handled properly or if the courts took an extremely conservative position on the meaning and entitlements of Section 1981.

I pressed my claims vigorously through my attorney and actually defeated General Motors. Shortly following the completion of the trial in Federal Court, I asserted the issue of entitlements, one entitlement being the issue of reinstatement.

"Bob, now that I've won my case, when do I get my job back?"

"Gary, you shouldn't want your job. You shouldn't want to go back."

"Why?"

"Because of the way they treated you."

"I know Bob. I know they treated me badly. However, that was my career, my fucking career. Don't you understand? I am entitled to get my job back under the law. It's my career."

"I know you are entitled to it, but the judge is not going to give it to you."

"Why won't he give it to me? What do you mean? You haven't even presented any arguments to Judge Gordon yet. How do you know what he's going to do?"

"He's just not going to do it. General Motors is hostile."

"Hostile? Yes, I know that. They cannot benefit from their own hostility. It's my entitlement under the law. And besides, you know I have yet to stabilize my employment as a direct result of this litigation with General Motors. I now have permanent career damage as a result of this. This is an even more pressing reason for you to get my job back. I have three kids and a wife to feed. My income has been adversely affected, you know."

"Gary, I still say you should not want to go back. You won your case against General Motors."

"Yeah, I know I won. However, I need you to get everything I'm entitled to and that includes all interest, my job and whatever else. Why do I always have to debate with you, Bob? What's with you? I don't understand. I'm trying to be nice to you, professional, cooperative, courteous. Tell me what's with you, huh?!"

"Well, you shouldn't want . . . ."

"Bob, the reinstatement is a very important issue to me and you can make it important to General Motors as well."

"Judge Gordon is not going to give it to you. I just know it."

"You knew I was going to lose also, didn't you?"

"Well, I thought . . . ."

"Bob, just press all the issues, will you? Maybe we can avoid General Motors appealing this thing and press for a settlement of some kind. Get back to me as soon as you can. This is very important to me and my family. Okay?"

"Yeah, Gary."

Several weeks passed, but I hadn't heard from Bob Gingras on the status of my entitlements. Shortly following this brief period I contacted Bob once again.

CHAPTER X

Judgment Day

Finally in March of 1991, Attorney Robert Gingras notified me that he arranged to have a hearing scheduled before Judge Gordon in April of 1991 on the issue of reinstatement to my former position, or an alternative one. If reinstatement was not possible, Judge Gordon would decide on the issue of front pay.

"Well Hon, I guess this is about the best news I've heard in a long time. It seems Bob has arranged to get a hearing conference scheduled with Judge Gordon sometime in April."

"I guess you've called him enough and written him enough letters over the years. What is the meeting for, anyway?"

"For resolution of the judgment I won against General Motors."

"Did Bob straighten that out yet? I thought you talked with him about that issue before."

"I have, but until he provides me with verbal feedback and written confirmation that he understands what I want, I have no choice except to constantly remind him of these things."

"Why don't you just give up?"

"Give up?! You've got to be kidding! I understand all this has taken a toll on you and the kids."

"It's also taken a toll on you, Gary. Look at you. You do many other things. You've worked for Wall Street companies and others, but you keep coming back to this trial with General Motors."

"I know. It's a rather unfortunate situation. I guess it's more than that. It's one hell of a dilemma, especially when Bob let my punitive and compensatory damages get away like that. I just don't understand how he allowed General Motors to do that. I told him!"

"All I know is this thing has been going on for a long, long time now."

"It doesn't have to, you know. If Bob would sit down with me and an expert on the damages done to my career as a result of this, we could file well-supported briefs regarding the issues remanded back to the District Court for Judge Gordon's decision. If we press these issues with General Motors' defense counsel, this case would be over!"

"Why doesn't he do what you say?"

"I don't know. I simply do not understand him at all. I don't know what's gotten into him. I should not have to tell him these things. After all, he keeps telling me he's the expert in these matters and that the courts under President Bush are very conservative. The courts are saying he forgot this and that."

"How's your back, Dear?"

"Well, I have some discomfort still. It seems to be getting better."

"Do you have to go back to the doctor again?"

"Yeah. Next week I'm scheduled for a follow-up with my primary physician, Dr. Diaz, on Tuesday morning and with Dr. Newman on Thursday evening."

"When will you be done with these back treatments?"

"Well, that depends on my prognosis which is being evaluated on a weekly basis. You know how they schedule things at the clinic, Hon. You're there for the kids yourself more than I am."

"Yeah, you're right, but they must have told you something about how long."

"I guess they don't know how long yet. My condition is being monitored."

"Hey, the weather is just perfect; it's fantastic. Why don't we take the kids to the Milwaukee County Zoo today? They'll just love that."

"I don't know. There are so many things we have to prepare."

"Call the kids. See if they want to go to the zoo or the museum . . . preferably the Zoo. It's a great day out."

"Gary, they're probably out playing somewhere."

"This early? We have plenty of time. Let them bring their friends too. There they are! Hey girls? Do you want to go to the zoo today, or would you rather go to the museum or take in a movie?"

"Let's go to the zoo today and a movie later, Dad. My class is scheduled to take us to the museum anyway."

"Okay, the zoo it is. I don't know when we're going to do all these other things because money is tight, but I'll see what I can do. Hon, pack some lunch, okay?"

"What do you want?"

"Just put together whatever you have and let's get out of here. The fresh air will do us some good. It's been a terribly cold winter, not much snow, but cold."

At this particular time of year the weather was very unpredictable. We'd have several days of warmth, making it difficult to determine what season it was. As soon as we'd get used to those warm days we'd get a sudden burst of Arctic air surging in from Canada.

Several weeks had now gone by. Each week I continued my employment search, looking for work similar to the work I had done at General Motors and for the Wall Street related firms. The economy was not in the best shape. In fact, the economic posture was rather bleak. This made my employment search very difficult. In addition, my involvement with General Motors Corporation was a major concern regarding my employment future. Generally, prospective employers have a tendency to frown on such involvements. This could be the single most factor in someone not offering a job. Prospective employers have their way of finding out these things. Employers seem not to be concerned about who started it. The employee is to take full responsibility for the involvement and, in fact, is perceived in a different light than everyone else. This is why it was so important for Bob Gingras to completely and effectively assert all claims and pursue all entitlements available under the statute in order to make me or anyone so similarly situated "whole."

Several more weeks went by and soon I received a phone call from Bob Gingras from his Madison office.

"Gary, this is Bob Gingras. Do you have a second?"

"Yeah, Bob. I'm still out of work, if that's your question, and have been for some time now."

"Yeah, Gary. I know."

"Bob, I just cannot understand how I could win my case and prove that my position was wrongfully terminated. Corporate procedures were not followed. I was subjected to harassment, and the person who terminated me did not have the authority. Previously, my performance was highly effective and outstanding. I simply cannot understand why I have to be without, do you?"

"Gary, that's why I'm calling you. Will you agree to a postponement of the remand hearing?"

"Postponement?! You have to be kidding. What is with you? Don't you think my family and I have been holding on long enough? I won my case against General Motors in 1988 before Judge Gordon and a Federal jury. Now it's 1991 and you want me to postpone? What is with you?!"

"Gary, you don't understand. Something has come up and I need a postponement."

"No, Bob. No postponement! I am losing my home because of this involvement. In fact, I've written several letters explaining this to you. I asked you to prepare a collection memorandum to collect what's left of the monetary side of the judgment in order to help mitigate the damages I experienced due to the delays in collecting my judgment to begin with."

"Gary, why don't you think about it?"

"Look, I've been cooperative with you, the courts, General Motors and everyone through this entire ordeal. At every level you seem to lose entitlements of mine. Why don't you get real? We need to close this out so I can get on with my life or whatever career I'll have afterwards."

"Gary, it would be better for everyone."

"Everyone except me, right? I've been litigating with General Motors for a long time now. I've beaten General Motors and now I expect to get what I'm entitled to receive under the statutes. Everything. As you know, General Motors' defense posture was rather malicious and nasty, and it may inflict irreparable and permanent career damage. My primary concern is that I have a rather large family to feed. I want you to recover and assert these permanent career damage claims against General Motors and anyone else who has caused these problems."

"I will, Gary."

"Bob, I've been a total gentleman throughout this process and have nothing to show for it. Do you want me to lose my home? My career has been permanently damaged. What else do you want to see? Let's get on with this thing as scheduled. This is 1991, Bob. Just move forward with the experts on my damages and collect my judgment and all other entitlements that I asked you back in 1988. Can you just do that, and get everything else I'm entitled to? Do you want me to talk to Judge Gordon myself, Bob?"

"No, Gary."

"Bob, get back to me. I have to go. Just press for the collection and keep the scheduled conference date. I have to go. My back is hurting."

"Are you still receiving back treatments, Gary?"

"Yeah, Bob. I have to go now. Get back to me on this thing. It is extremely important you handle the reinstatement issue carefully. Brief the issue and ask Judge Gordon if he will hear expert testimony on that issue. It is extremely important you handle this properly. I cannot stress it any more than what I am saying to you."

"I know."

"I've been through a lot. I shouldn't have to explain that to you. I am trying to cooperate with you fully. Do you understand me, Bob?"

"Yes, Gary. You don't have to tell me. I understand. I am an expert."

"I respect that you're a recognized expert in this field. It's just at times it seems these things are not important to you. Just stay focused on the issues of the matters before the court and required procedures. I have to go now."

CHAPTER XI

Congressional Intent

In 1964, the United States Congress passed the Civil Rights Act, which was signed by President Lyndon B. Johnson. This legislation provided additional protection and addressed other public policy issues not specifically covered by the Civil Rights Statutes of 1866 and 1874, better known as Section 1981.

In 1990, the United States Congress again introduced additional legislation for more advanced worker protection of protected classes, determining that existing legislation in this particular area was not complete. President George Bush did not agree with several aspects of the proposed legislation as drafted by Congress and, therefore, did not approve it in that form. President Bush rejected the Bill and sent it back to Congress for further development.

In the meantime, many litigants were either in court or before Department of Labor agencies in an attempt to resolve their differences. This kind of legislation had a significant impact on the State and Federal Courts in terms of providing direction to the Court, showing the intent of Congress, granting entitlements, and determining violations of a person's rights under the statute. This is extremely important legislation as mandated by the United States Congress and enforced by the Department of Labor agencies and the U.S. Courts.

The United States Supreme and Appellate Courts, as well as the Federal District Court and State Courts, fashion their decisions on the intent and meaning of the statutes. If the statutes are vaguely written and the meaning and intent of the statutes are not clear, then the courts are free to decide accordingly. The result of the court's decision could even be perceived as tremendously unfair, almost completely neutralizing the meaning of the statute itself. This is an extremely important domestic issue to further enhance harmony and advancement of those workers in America who are so protected.

The United States Congress understood the importance of such a Bill for Civil Rights in order to correct the wrongs of individuals so adversely affected. The U.S. Supreme Court further interpreted the meaning of Section 1981 as it related to the Patterson case. They interpreted the statute as pertaining to the initial formation of contract, which means conduct during the initial hire. This interpretation is rather significant because it is the essence of the damage claims allowed under the statute. The McKnight v. General Motors matter was on appeal and had completed trial before the U.S. District Court for the Eastern District of Wisconsin when the U.S. Supreme Court decided Patterson v. McClean Credit Union, 491 U.S. 164,176 (1989).

More specifically, compensatory and punitive damages are recoverable under Section 1981, Civil Rights Bill of 1866. These damages were not available for litigants whose injuries occurred after the initial employment offer and hire. Many cases litigated and won under the statute were later adversely affected by the U.S. Supreme Court ruling, providing the Appellate Courts and District Courts below did not recognize cases to be excluded from the ruling, and providing the appropriate waivers were in place. It seemed the courts were following a very conservative and narrow posture.

It was the intent of Congress, as referenced in the Senate Conference Report, H.R. 1746, 118 of the Congressional Record 7166, 7168 of 1972, concerning Section 706q, that the provisions of this section were intended to provide the courts broad discretion in carrying out their equitable authority to provide victims of such unlawfulness the most complete remedy possible. The Congressional Record further required an aggrieved person, caused by the consequences and effects of an unlawful employment practice, be restored to a position where they would have been were it not for the unlawful occurrence.

The United States Congress's intent is further supported and outlined in additional proposed legislation to improve existing civil rights statutes. As referenced above, the courts have discretionary power to grant a "make whole" remedy, and it should not be refused. Discretion is merely given to the courts to make the most complete resolve of the objectives of Title VII, that which is so attainable.

In effect, Congress provided the courts with the latitude of taking a thorough look at what damages have been borne by the aggrieved party and providing complete remedy to restoration.

Throughout my entire legal bout with General Motors, it often appeared as if Congressional and U.S. Supreme Court law intended one purpose while everyone else wanted to do something vastly different. One could rightfully conclude that although Congress developed legislation to handle certain issues, the courts don't necessarily comply with it.

With regard to remedies for plaintiffs who experienced an egregious or wrongful act in violation of the statute, the courts were growing more conservative in restoring fully or providing appropriate remedy to the aggrieved party. Even though it appeared the judicial environment was becoming more conservative, it was important to continue to thrust forward and press the issues which were not as controversial. However, in a conservative environment, even clear issues can become controversial. Even the word conservative means many things to many people.

The U.S. Supreme Court reinterpreted the meaning of Section 1981 as it pertains to the Civil Rights Statute passed by the U.S. Congress in 1866. It clarified the meaning of Section 1981 in its decision of Patterson v. McClean Credit Union, 491 U.S. 164, 176 (1989). The U.S. Supreme Court decision indicated that the decision pertained to the conduct of the employer during the initial hire of the employee and not the conduct which occurred following the initial formation and making of the contract. This decision affected court awards which were pending regarding the compensatory and punitive damage claims and awards. In effect, the decision provided that compensatory and punitive damage claims were not available under Section 1981 for the aggrieved.

This created an even more pressing need for Congress and the President of the United States to develop and implement an effective Civil Rights Statute in order to provide reasonable remedies to the aggrieved parties. However, Congress and President Bush could not completely agree on the complexion that the new Civil Rights Bill should take. Several court awarded judgments suffered adversely, as did the plaintiffs who had prevailed under the old law.

The U.S. Supreme Court provided exception to applying the law retroactively, leaving it to the discretion of the courts to determine if appropriate waivers and exceptions had been filed.

CHAPTER XII

Summary Judgment

"It is a tragedy and gross disrespect when deception outweighs the necessity of understanding the importance of interpreting the meaning of the principles of law as established by our forefathers and the common good of those who genuinely apply themselves to fashion law to harness the rights of those embodied and expressed in the Constitution."

—Gary McKnight

Unlawful conduct deliberately perpetrated against another is indeed injurious. In general, to correct the wrongs and recover for the injuries caused to anyone is to rest with confidence with those who have the authority to interpret and apply the principles which so govern.

Consider the following excerpts of well established case law, keeping in mind the intent of Congress as expressed in Subsection 706(g) is to give the courts the power to exercise broad discretion in delivering their equitable powers to fashion the most complete remedy possible in fully restoring those affected. Discretion is merely vested to the trial court in order to allow the most complete achievement and advancement of the principle objectives of the provisions of the statute.

The objective is to provide the "make whole" remedy, to fully restore the person affected by the unlawful conduct as expressed in Albermarle Paper Company v. Moody (Nos. 74-389 and 74-428 10 FEP Cases 1181, 422 U.S. 405 (1975), Supreme Court Decision, June 25, 1975. The legislature required reinstatement of an employee by a private employer once proven unlawful.

The unlawfully affected individual under the relevant statutes should be placed in the position he would have enjoyed if it had not been for the unlawful conduct as expressed in Rios v. Enterprise Association Steamfitters Local 638 of UA 501 F2d 622 (1974).

It is required to provide the developmental requirements to victims subjected to unlawful conduct expressed under the relevant statute as in Franks v. Bowman Transportation Company, U.S. Court of Appeals Fifth Circuit (New Orleans),

495 F2d 398 (1974), reviewed by the U.S. Supreme Court. It was decided that the unlawfully discharged employee was entitled to constructive seniority. The U.S. Supreme Court held that the legislative policy was in favor of restoring fully the unlawfully terminated employee under the relevant statute.

During Chief Justice Burger's term in the U.S. Supreme Court, he stated where retroactive seniority is not available, an award of front pay could replace the need for competitive seniority.

In White v. Carolina Paper Board Corporation, EPD (W.D. NC 1974) Judge McMillian found a pervasive policy and practice of unlawful conduct and ordered front pay or some other form of prospective remedy until the aggrieved individuals were assigned better employment. There are many other such cases where a reasonable remedy for the aggrieved has been secured.

In an opinion expressed in the Kurle case, citing Sampson v. Murray, 415 U.S. sec. 96 415 U.S. 61 N68 (1974), it was determined that if harm warranted reinstatement of public employees, the same harm justified reinstatement of private employees. The U.S Supreme Court held that such harm warrants preliminary injunctive remedy.

Furthermore, the trial court in McMullan v. Thorburgh ordered reinstatement even though the office had been filled subsequent to the unlawful discharge. The trial court here held that the wrongfully terminated employee had a superior claim to reinstatement. (McMullan v. Thorburgh, 508 F.Supp. 1044 (E.D. Pa 1981).)

It was held in Brokmeyer v. Dun & Bradstreet, 113 Wis. 2d.561, 335 N.W. 2d 834 (1983), that reinstatement and back pay are the most appropriate remedies in the interest of public policy for unlawful termination.

It appears that a substantial majority of the entitlements espoused under the statutes are not entitlements which are mandatory or automatic. The trial court judge has wide discretion in exercising his equitable powers to fashion the most complete remedy. The Congressional statute which governs and grants such authority to the trial judge requires full restoration to a position where the aggrieved would have been were it not for the unlawful violation of the statute, as referenced in the U.S. Senate Conference Report concerning Section 706(g).

In matters regarding equity as no place else, courts have developed absolutes and have evaluated the realities and necessities involved in providing some level of reconciliation for competing interest as expressed in Lemon v. Kurtzman, 411 U.S. 192, 201 (1973) in the opinion of Chief Justice Burger.

The previously referenced cases and opinions are but a few of the well established cases to fully carry the intent of Congress and that of the U.S. Supreme Court as expressed in the decision concerning Albermarle Paper Company v. Moody ("making whole" the aggrieved individuals) and Franks v. Bowman Transportation Company (fully restoring them to their rightful place).

The failure to grant seniority or reinstatement is an unlawful act as defined under statute Section 703(h) because it perpetuates the effects of pre-act conduct as previously defined, as is the opinion of U.S. Supreme Court Chief Justice Rehnquist.

Although I prevailed in Federal District Court against the General Motors Corporation, my judgment was eventually retested by the massive automotive company as a new slate of principles emerged after the U.S. Supreme Court Decision of Patterson v. McLean Credit Union. It held that Section 1981 concerned itself with conduct occurring during the initial making and enforcement of contract, the initial hire, and did not concern itself with such conduct thereafter.

The United States Court of Appeals for the Seventh Circuit, which pondered whether General Motors had waived its right to invoke Patterson by not raising the argument before them, concluded I had waived the defense of waiver since my counsel never argued that General Motors waived its right to rely on Patterson (McKnight v. General Motors Corporation, 908 F2d 104, 110-11, Seventh Circuit 1990).

A motion for summary judgment is an application to a court or judge for the immediate determination or adjudication of the rights and entitlements of the parties to an action. In earlier discussions, I encouraged Bob Gingras to address General Motors' appellate issues accordingly in case General Motors decided to appeal, which eventually they did.

The Appellate Court and the U.S. Supreme Court procedures are separate from those of the trial court below, although relative to a common thread regarding the interpretation and application of the law.

Although the U.S. District Court below entered judgement in my favor as determined in the trial court thereof, its determination was subject to an appeal, if General Motors could establish a basis for the right to an appeal. It was up to the giant General Motors Corporation and their team of lawyers to dismantle that which was entered in my favor in the trial court below.

The issue of reinstatement was denied by the trial judge, the Honorable Myron Gordon, on the grounds that General Motors was hostile; the parties were acrimonious; the plaintiff expressed alternative positions when he could not get his original position back. He also took into consideration the size of the verdict given me against General Motors, a verdict which had not become final as General Motors did indeed have appellate rights after verdict. These issues set the tone of the appeal in this matter.

The relevant testimony at trial provided that my performance was more than acceptable. In fact, the performance which survived the trial was that I was rated highly effective and outstanding with projected indications that I would attain a much higher level of position than the one I occupied at the time of the unlawful discharge. Additional testimony showed I possessed strong management skills and conducted myself professionally. It was determined that my termination was wrongful; corporate procedures were not followed. The person who terminated me did not have complete authority to do so. The jury concurred that my termination from GM was motivated by unlawful conduct as expressed under Title VII and that General Motors violated the statute. The Federal jury did not know my reinstatement and/or front pay entitlements would be in jeopardy at the time they concluded their determinations. The issue of reinstatement was a determination of the trial judge and my attorney.

Again it seemed as if the United Auto Workers Union employees had superior claims regarding their particular employment rights compared to that of General Motors Corporation management personnel. When a Union worker is wrongfully terminated, he is often given his position back when an unfair labor practice is determined.

Chapter XIII

Final Determinations

The summer of 1991 was fast approaching, but the matter involving General Motors continued. The parties involved in the legal bout were even more frustrated with the intricacies and realities of the matter before the court.

In the meantime, I was recovering from a back and ligament injury sustained because a manager for a different employer required me to frequently engage in maneuvering heavy merchandise. I zealously attempted to do many things during the pendency of my rightful claims before the Eastern District Court of Wisconsin. McKnight was deeply entrenched in other legal strife as a direct result of his involvement with the General Motors court case on the grounds of rather substantial representations made by Bob Gingras.

Throughout the pendency of the legal issues which were before the U.S. Appellate Court for the Seventh Circuit and the U.S. Supreme Court, I often engaged in communication with Bob Gingras regarding matters concerning any additional damages which might be recoverable as a result of the trial and tactical delays which kept the litigation going. I discussed with Bob the importance of complete recovery. He frequently reassured me that he was fully aware of what was required, that everything was being handled and that all remaining claims were being addressed properly.

"Dad, here's your mail."

"Why thank you, Honey. Oh, Kim? I know you're only trying to be helpful by bringing Daddy the mail, but I'd rather you not do that."

"Why not, Daddy?"

"Well, our mail box is away from the house, right next to the main road and an awful lot of cars come by. They travel very fast and I don't want you getting the mail until you're a little bit older. You have to pay attention to the cars passing when you're getting the mail."

"I do, Daddy."

"Well let's play it safe and let me or your mother get the mail for now. Where are your sisters?"

"Cassandra's outside with Jenny and Amanda, and Felicia is upstairs in her room."

"Where are you going now?"

"I'm going outside to play with Jacob and Emily. Come get me when Bridget gets here."

Kim is my youngest daughter who was born around the time of my near-miss accident with the brother of one of the defendants in the McKnight v. General Motors court case and shortly before my termination from General Motors.

When I looked at the mail, I found letters from my attorney out East and from Robert Gingras. I opened Bob's letter first. He requested me to call him to talk about the issues for our hearing next week before Judge Myron Gordon. I couldn't believe there was a hearing scheduled for the next week. He didn't even mention the experts. What was he doing? I called his office immediately.

"Gingras and Schaefer. Can I help you?"

"Yes. Is Attorney Bob Gingras in?"

"Who's calling?"

"Gary McKnight."

"May I ask what this is in reference to?"

"Yes, it's in reference to his letter asking me to call him."

"Hold on," she said, then, "Bob must have stepped out of his office. I'll have him return your call."

Several hours passed. It was getting closer to the end of the work day. If he didn't call by 4:00 p.m. I decided I'd call him again. Soon the phone rang.

"Gary? This is Bob Gingras."

"Yes, Bob. How are you? I've been waiting for your call."

"Good. Did you get my letter?"

"Yes. That's what prompted me to call you, but I guess I would have called you anyway had you not sent me the letter."

"Gary, we have a hearing scheduled with Judge Gordon next week on the issues remanded by the United States Court of Appeals."

"Yes, I see that Bob."

"Do you have any questions, Gary?"

"Well, yes. I don't understand what you're doing."

"What do you mean?"

"Well, I've had several conversations with you on how I'd like you to handle the remaining issues before Judge Gordon, but I don't see any effort on your part here that you've done that."

"I understand your concern, however, it's not required for us to approach it that way yet."

"You don't know that Bob. You don't know what Judge Gordon is going to require or do."

"Yeah, I do."

"Well, I'm not going to argue with you. You know the courts are extremely conservative in their rulings and unpredictable. I just think we ought to set the pace here. Just lay the foundation and establish our presence. I think what you should do is first brief the issues of reinstatement and front pay, as well as other damage issues and offer expert testimony on these matters. These issues are rather important to me."

"Gary, that's not required."

"Fine. You keep telling me you're the expert on this issue. I just think what I am suggesting is not at all far-fetched!"

"Gary, I'll handle it."

"Bob, this is our last and best chance at recovering these things, and indeed they have significant value. Bob, I'm done with it, but I want you to file a brief on those issues and engage an expert to explain thoroughly to Judge Gordon the issues that should be considered in his final determination. I hope you're . . . you just have to be ready. Bob, I've got to go."

"Where do you want to meet next week?"

"Let's meet in the lounge of the Pfister Hotel across from the Federal building at 8:00 a.m."

"Fine. I'll see you then."

Once again I found myself back before Judge Myron Gordon, Senior Federal Judge of the Eastern District of Wisconsin. I held a discussion with Bob Gingras about the issues on remand before Judge Gordon in the dining room of the Milwaukee Pfister Hotel, one of Milwaukee's finest establishments and much a part of Wisconsin history.

"Well, we're finally going back before Judge Gordon with regard to my entitlements as remanded from the U.S. Court of Appeals for the Seventh Circuit. It's about time. Don't you think so, Bob?"

"Yeah, it is," Bob said.

"Well, Bob, the reason I am somewhat impatient at this time is that because of this involvement, I am about to lose my home. It has been quite some time now since I won my case against General Motors. I won my case in 1988 and it is now 1991. Don't you think that's a long time to be waiting for your entitlements from a case?"

"Well . . . ."

"Never mind, Bob. Let's talk about the matter before us now. I'd like you to retain an expert or ask Judge Gordon if you can have an expert go before him with regard to my career damages and any other damages I may have experienced as a result of this involvement. Just take a look at it, will you?"

"Gary, do you want to go back to General Motors?"

"Bob, I just told you I'm losing my home, didn't I? My job entitlement issue is one thing of value left in this case. You need to handle it very carefully. Now, to answer your question . . . yes."

"Then, Gary, we'll have to ask Judge Gordon for your job."

"Bob, this is more complex than just asking him for my job. I am entitled to full restoration of my career, which is more than the job I lost. Just work with an expert, a career specialist, on the issue. This is our last chance."

"What position do you want, Gary?"

"What position am I entitled to? Just ask Judge Gordon if an expert could provide an opinion on this matter."

"Gary, I am an expert."

"Bob, this is a complex issue. You don't know every position that General Motors has."

"I am an expert on this."

"Okay, Bob. I just want to make certain you handle this properly. You keep talking to me about President Bush and his administration and the courts . . . how conservative they are. All I want you to do is handle this properly. Get a career specialist to testify. This and the front pay issue are all we have left."

We proceeded across Wisconsin Avenue into the Federal Courthouse Building.

"What is this? Security inspection? When was all this security equipment installed? Go ahead, Bob. You walk through the security screen first."

On my way through, the alarm went off. Beep . . . beep . . . beep . . . beep. Security got up and asked me to remove what metal I had in my pockets and go through again. I handed over my keys and went through again. The alarm did not go off, so we proceeded directly to Judge Myron Gordon's courtroom. The defense attorneys arrived shortly afterward.

Judge Gordon made his presence, and it was so quiet in the courtroom you could almost hear a pin drop. Judge Gordon quickly addressed the issues before him, asking the attorneys on both sides if either wished to file a brief on the matter before the court. Both responded they did not.

In the meantime, I was sitting at the plaintiff's table looking up at the judge, shaking my head up and down with regard to his question on the brief. I was also trying to get Bob to come over to the plaintiff's table to talk about this brief issue, but he continued making statements before the court and the judge.

Afterward, the judge allowed us to leave the courtroom. In the meantime, I operated as professionally as I could, trying not to explode before the court and be found in contempt. It was very important that I did not lose my composure here. Somehow I managed to come out of Judge Gordon's courtroom without going into the details of my concerns with Bob, but not for long.

We continued our journey through the corridors of the Federal Courthouse Facility, and I could feel my frustrations building inside. I tried to contain them, but I could hold them in no longer.

"Bob! What is with you?! Judge Gordon asked you if you wanted to file a brief! What are you doing?!"

"Gary, calm down."

"Bob! I could lose my home here! Get on with this. File the brief! Besides, it's been about three years since I won my case against General Motors, not two as you told Judge Gordon! Almost three! Just file the brief, okay?"

"Gary, Judge Gordon knows what's before him."

"Bob. I don't want to tell you how to do your job. You keep telling me President Bush, his administration and the appointed judges are conservative! The results here so far are contrary to that of the U.S. Supreme Court and Congressional meaning. Conservative?"

"They are, Gary."

"Bob, I just want you to press forward with the issues in my case. File the brief. The courthouse security staff is standing over there. Let's go. I don't want to get upset. I have been cooperative with you throughout this entire involvement. Just try to get on with this issue. Why are you taking so long? It is easier for you to get these entitlements before Judge Gordon in District Court than to take it back up again. Besides, these are things the U.S. Supreme Court and the U.S. Congress say I am entitled to under the statute. Bob, I have to go. Get back to me on this and the other matters."

*   *   *

In July of 1991, Judge Gordon handed down his decision and order on remand. He indicated he was surprised neither party wished to file a brief on the remand issues before him. He decided that since a brief had not been filed he would refer to the trial record. Judge Gordon decided I would not be entitled to reinstatement on the grounds that I have different career interests, as shown by the kind of work I held when working for Wall Street related firms. The trial judge further denied me any front pay as available under the statute on the grounds that back in 1988 the jury did not provide remedy for loss of future earning capacity. The trial judge denied pre-interest in the judgment of back pay on the grounds that the request for it was entered late. The trial judge upheld the portion of the judgment that pertained to the back pay award. The section 1981 claim which did not survive the Patterson decision was dismissed.

Attorney Robert Gingras was encouraged to appeal the entire decision and order on remand as it did not appear to conform to the statute or its intent.

In August of 1991, Gingras went before the trial judge himself, with opposing counsel for the defendant General Motors. By September 9, 1991, I received a letter of withdrawal from Robert Gingras. A brief was due before the Seventh Circuit U.S. Court of Appeals in Chicago on October 4, 1991. Therefore, I filed a motion to represent myself, and requested an extension of time.

In the meantime, I interviewed additional attorneys to continue the litigation. Most agreed to represent me initially, but indicated they would have to talk with Bob Gingras. Whether they did or not, they said they would. Shortly afterward, they decided not to take my case, in spite of the fact significant legal issues and value remained. This matter of litigation was indeed a classic case in itself . . . the type of case most lawyers would relish. In fact, this case had already been won! At this point, the matter simply involved getting those things that I, as the plaintiff, was entitled to by the statute.

I contacted the State Bar Associations in Wisconsin and Illinois. I also made several trips to the Milwaukee County Library to complete my research on the selection of replacement counsel using the Martindale Hubble, a reference source which provides information on lawyers.

I selected two attorneys to continue the litigation against General Motors and their tremendous legal staff. John Williamson, Jr., who attended Columbia and Yale Universities, would be one of the replacements; and Edna Selan, who attended Howard and the University of Chicago would be the other lawyer. (By no means does the selection here pass judgment on the credentials of the many fine educational institutions of this country or the ability of an attorney.)

In November of 1991, the United States Congress passed the Civil Rights Bill, later signed by the President. Although the Circuit Courts remained conservative, the courts were divided on how the 1991 law would affect cases that were filed and pending before passage, an issue which has not been resolved by the courts at this time.

In December of 1992, I prepared and filed pro se a Petition for a Writ of Certiorari to the United States Court of Appeals for the Seventh Circuit in the United States Supreme Court for the issues that remained and had been decided upon previously.

During the latter part of December of 1992, I filed another Petition for a Writ of Certiorari to the U.S. Court of Appeals for the Seventh Circuit in the United States Supreme Court for the matter of the section 1981 issue on the damages of the case in relation to the 1991 law passed by Congress and signed by President Bush in the fall of 1991.

General Motors defense attorneys continued their thrust with regard to this litigation.

> "There should follow others who possess great knowledge and depth, as the Honorable Supreme Court Justice Thurgood Marshall, as to understand the purpose and consequences of the law. For those who fail to follow the principle meaning of the United States Constitution cast in jeopardy the foundation of their country."
>
> Gary McKnight

In October of 1992, General Motors Corporation, for the first time in its corporate history, orchestrated the shakeup of its management ranks as a result of unparalleled record losses in its North American operations.

In February of 1993, the United States Supreme Court decided to resolve the issue of whether the Civil Rights Bill of 1991 would have retroactive status, a matter to be concluded later this year. The majority of the Appellate Circuit Courts below have decided that the law is not retroactive.

Although McKnight's case before the court has been greatly fragmented by this time, the Supreme Court is the final threshold for recovery, if there is to be any recovery at all.

As of April 1993, the issue has still not been decided and the saga of McKnight v. General Motors Corporation continues . . . a bout to be reckoned.

UNITED STATES DISTRICT COURT
EASTERN DISTRICT OF WISCONSIN

GARY McKNIGHT, Plaintiff

v.

GENERAL MOTORS CORPORATION, Defendant.

Case No. 87-C-248

DECISION AND ORDER ON REMAND

In 1988, Gary McKnight prevailed on his claim that the defendant, General Motors Corporation, unlawfully discharged him from his employment because of his race and in retaliation for his prior complaints of race discrimination. Mr. McKnight pressed his case under Title VII of the Civil Rights Act of 1964, 42 U.S.C. sec. 2000e et seq., and 42 U.S.C. sec. 1981, which is based on the Civil Rights Act of 1866. A jury heard his sec. 1981 claim, and this court resolved the Title VII dispute. Judgment was entered in the plaintiff's favor in the amount $610,000.00, plus attorney's fees. Specifically, the jury awarded $55,000.00 in back pay, another $55,000.00 for emotional distress, and $500,000.00 as punitive damages.

This court denied Mr. McKnight's post-trial motion for reinstatement to his former position as a manufacturing supervisor and his alternative request for reinstatement to a different job in a different location but still within the General Motors Corp., 705 F. Supp. 464 (E.D. Wis. 1989). The defendant appealed the judgment except for the award of attorney's fees, and the plaintiff appealed that portion of the judgment denying reinstatement.

During the pendency of the appeal, the United States Supreme Court decided Patterson v. McLean Credit Union, 491 U.S 164, 176 (1989), which holds that sec. 1981 was limited to providing redress for unlawful discrimination in the

---

143

"making and enforcement of private contacts," and specifically held that sec. 1981 afforded no relief from "problems that may arise later from the conditions of continuing employment."

On appeal, the court of appeals for the seventh circuit decided that Patterson should be applied retroactively. McKnight v. General Motors Corp., 908 F.2d 104, 110-11 (7th Cir. 1990). The court of appeals directed me to dismiss Mr. McKnight's sec. 1981 claims. The court also remanded "for reconsideration of his entitlement to reinstatement (or in lieu thereof to front pay) under Title VII." Id. at 117.

The first issue raised here by the parties is the scope of consideration on remand. The defendant urges that the reconsideration is limited to the record as it stands; the plaintiff argues that the court should reopen the record to receive additional evidentiary submissions on the questions of reinstatement and front pay.

The instructions from the court of appeals do not expressly or impliedly call for additional evidence. The court's instructions are "to reexamine the issue of reinstatement in light of [the vacation of the punitive damage award] and also in light of our discussion in the preceding paragraph of the circumstances in which denial of reinstatement is appropriate," McKnight, 908 F.2d at 116. The court also stated that "on remand the district court may wish to consider not only whether McKnight should be reinstated but also whether, if not, he can and should receive front pay in lieu of reinstatement." Id. at 117.

Mr. McKnight argues that the change in the law occasioned by the Patterson decision had "obvious corresponding impacts on matters litigated in this case," Plaintiff's brief in opposition at p. 2. Patterson in no way changed the remedies available under Title VII. Reinstatement and front pay were available when the case was tried and still remain possible remedies under Title VII.

I also reject the plaintiff's contention that his current employment situation must be explored in order to resolve the remanded matters. The record was fully established as of the end of the trial, unless there exists a contrary instruction from the appellate court. I cannot find such an instruction in the court of appeals' ruling. Mr. McKnight made his record regarding damages both past and future, during the trial, and he submitted his case regarding reinstatement in post-trial briefs.

A status conference was held in open court on May 16, 1991. At that time, I heard the parties' positions as to the remanded issues and inquired of the parties whether they wanted to file written memoranda further addressing the issues of reinstatement and front pay. Surprisingly, both sides declined. The defendant did ask for and did receive an opportunity to brief the issue of attorney's fees. The briefs on that one issue have been filed, and the issues remanded by the court of appeals are now ripe for review.

With reference to "the record" in this case, I am constrained to observe that the court of appeals addressed a matter of "trial error" that it acknowledged was not a part of the record. Indeed, it was a matter that the court of appeals expressly recognized was not preserved for appeal and had been waived. Nevertheless, the panel concluded that because of the time limitations which I set, the defendant's witnesses actually "ran" to and from the witness stand. This, the court of appeals stated, created a "spectacle" and a "relay race." It was "unseemly," the court of appeals went on to note, McKnight, 908 F.2d at 115.

Unfortunately, in going dehors the record, the court of appeals unfairly relied on the partisan representation of General Motors' disappointed trial counsel, whose prized client had suffered an adverse jury verdict of over $600,000. The appellate court's reliance was enhanced because Mr. McKnight's counsel understandably did not contradict that representation. Why, I ask, should plaintiff's counsel expend his valuable, restricted time to respond to an issue that was not preserved for appeal? He had to address other issues—ones based on the record—before his red light went on.

I have been a judge of a court of record for 40 years. In no instance, including the McKnight case, has a witness ever entered my courtroom on the run or exited from the witness stand at such a pace in a matter over which I have presided. The "unseemly spectacle" described in Judge Posner's decision simply did not take place. There was no "relay race."

The court of appeals also asserted that my time limits were imposed "arbitrarily." My decision to set time limitations stemmed from the following circumstances: On March 5, 1987, this case was filed and was assigned to Judge Thomas J. Curran; he entered a scheduling order on July 20, 1987, in which he stated that the time necessary for trial was "a maximum of three days." Subsequently, the case was randomly reassigned to Judge J.P. Stadtmueller. When I then volunteered to handle it in place of Judge Stadtmueller, the case was about a year and a half old and, on its face, it was an uncomplicated employment discrimination case which should be tried in a maximum of three days.

I conducted a pretrial conference on August 8, 1988, and set the trial to start on October 3, 1988. However, as the two sides geared up for trial, I found that they were crossing swords at every turn. Representing General Motors, the defense team was playing hardball; Mr. McKnight's counsel was equally out for blood. During the rather short period between the pretrial conference and the start of the trial, the volume of filings in this case more than doubled. General Motors submitted an inordinately large number of in limine motions seeking to exclude testimony from various witnesses. For instance, in reference to the deposition of one witness alone, Jacob Johnson, the defendant asked me to resolve over 65 evidentiary objections in advance of trial. Five days before the trial date, the defendant filed a motion for reconsideration of Judge Curran's denial of its motion for summary judgment. His decision on the original motion had been entered on May 12, 1988.

Being unable to agree on the questions to be included in a special verdict, counsel filed widely divergent proposals. They also vigorously disagreed on their proposed substantive jury instructions and submitted separate ones. There were 105 exhibits to be offered in evidence, and pretrial objections were advanced as to most of them.

As the trial date neared, I became increasingly aware of the extraordinary combativeness of counsel. I was firmly convinced that they were turning an acorn into an oak tree right before my eyes. It was my studied opinion that this case could fairly be tried in one week; it would needlessly have taken far longer than that if counsel had a free rein. After discussing this problem with counsel, I set the time limits. No objections were heard. The time limitations were calmly and deliberately set to meet a clearly demonstrated need; they were not "arbitrarily" imposed. I was fully mindful of the admonitions in Flaminio v. Honda Motor Co., Ltd., 733 F.2d 463 (1984) in setting the time restrictions in advance of the trial and in keeping them flexible as the trial progressed. It is regrettable that the court of appeals elected to buy the version of how this trial was conducted that was sold by General Motors' lawyer. With that said, I turn to the issues at hand.

I. REINSTATEMENT

The Title VII remedies in a particular case are to be fashioned in such a way as to return the victim of discrimination to the position he would have been in but for the illegal behavior, Albemarle Paper Co. v. Moody, 422 U.S. 405, 418-19 (1975). Reinstatement is not a tool to be used by an individual to fulfill his, as yet, unmet employment goals.

The court is to exercise its discretion so as to remedy the discrimination suffered by Mr. McKnight. One such potential remedy is reinstating Mr. McKnight to his former position. This remedy is in keeping with Albemarle. However, the remedy sought by Mr. McKnight is to be placed within General Motors in an entirely different job and to be relocated to a new city; that is his clear preference.

"A hiring order is not appropriate unless the person discriminated against is presently qualified to assume the position sought," Kamberos v. GTE Automatic Electric, Inc., 603 F.2d 598, 603 (7th Cir. 1979) (citing Franks v. Bowman Transportation Co., Inc., 424 U.S. 747 (1976)). Likewise, reinstatement is not warranted where the position sought is no longer available, Gaddy v. Abex

Corp., 884 F.2d 312, 319 (7th Cir. 1989). The case at bar does not involve a discriminatory failure to hire or a discriminatory firing disguised as an elimination of position or a reduction in force. However, the underlying policy is still the same: reinstatement must be feasible. There is no basis to find that Mr. McKnight is presently qualified to assume his preferred position in "corporate finance or investment banking" or that General Motors has such a position available.

The court of appeals' decision surmised that the plaintiff's desire to be reinstated might be motivated by his wish to be bought out, McKnight 908 F.2d at 116. This is not beyond the realm of possibility, especially in light of Mr. McKnight's changed career goals. Given Mr. McKnight's unequivocal desire to be in an entirely different field, reinstatement to his former position is not desirable or realistic.

Mr. McKnight could be reinstated to his former position as a manufacturing supervisor. Would the purposes of Title VII be advanced by such an order? I think not. Mr. McKnight's career goals and aspirations, as presented by his testimony at trial and through his experts, no longer include supervising the manufacture of automobile parts. He wants to be in the financial services industry. Title VII would not be served by placing the plaintiff in a job he does not want. Such a situation would likely cause Mr. McKnight to suffer again from emotional distress. This type of reaction "would ensue independently of any hostility or retaliation by the employer." Id.

I am directed to reexamine the issue of reinstatement in light of the fact that the punitive damage award and the compensatory damage award have been vacated. I do not believe that those circumstances change the equation. As stated in the original decision, a primary consideration in denying reinstatement was Mr. McKnight's express desire to work in another field. In ruling on the motions after judgment, I stated in the opinion published at 705 F. Supp. at 469:

After balancing all the equities, I am convinced that reinstatement in this case would not advance the purposes of Title VII. The plaintiff asserts that he prefers not to be reinstated in his former position of manufacturing supervisor but rather in a position concerned with corporate finance or investment banking. Further, the evidence at trial established that the plaintiff has changed his career goal from manufacturing management to being a stockbroker. I conclude that the plaintiff does not have a primary interest in the position that he formerly held.

That aspect of the case has not been altered by my reconsideration of the issue on this remand. The matters of compensatory and punitive damages awarded for his sec. 1981 claim, as well as the "acrimonious" employer-employee relationship, were viewed as lesser considerations; I still view them as such.

II. FRONT PAY

Is front pay an available remedy under Title VII? Yes, Weaver v. Casa Gallardo, Inc., 922 F.2d 1515, 1528 (11th Cir. 1991); Carter v. Sedgwick County, Kansas, 929 F.2d 1501, 1505 (10th Cir.1991); Edward v. Occidental Chemical Corp., 892 F.2d 1442, 1449 (9th Cir. 1990); Shore v. Federal Express Corp., 777 F.2d 1155, 1159 (6th Cir. 1985). This list, while certainly not exhaustive, is representative of the jurisdictions which hold that front pay is available under Title VII when reinstatement is denied.

Is an award of front pay appropriate in the case at bar? No. Mr. McKnight presented evidence to the jury regarding his employment future. The jury reasonably found that Mr. McKnight did not lose future earnings as a result of the discrimination he suffered at the hands of the defendant. Mr. McKnight earned considerably more money after his termination from General Motors. I am persuaded that Mr. McKnight's employment opportunities were not and are not inferior to his employment at General Motors.

III. ATTORNEY'S FEES

After the resolution of the post-trial motions, but before the issuance of the appellate mandate, the parties entered into a stipulation regarding the plaintiff's attorney's fees and costs. Pursuant to that stipulation, this court entered an order amending the judgment to add an award of $57,125.70 as attorney's fees and costs. Although the defendant did not appeal this aspect of the judgment, it now seeks to have the attorney's fee award reduced.

I do not consider it appropriate to revisit the attorney's fees award. The United States Supreme Court has stated:

> When a case has been once decided by this court on appeal, and remanded to the Circuit Court, whatever was before this court, and disposed of by its decree, is considered as finally settled. The Circuit Court is bound by the decree as the law of the case, and must carry it into execution, according to the mandate. That court cannot vary it, or examine it for any other purpose than execution; or give any other or further relief; or review it, even for apparent error, upon any matter decided on appeal; or intermeddle with it, further than to settle so much as has been remanded.

In re Sanford Fork & Tool Co., 160 U.S. 247, 255 (1895).

A lower court may decide matters left open by the mandate. Id. However, the issue of attorney's fees was not left open by the mandate of the court of appeals. How could it have been left open when the issue was not raised on appeal?

Even if I revisited the issue of attorney's fees, I would not disturb the stipulation previously entered by the parties. The amount of attorney's fees and costs was entirely reasonable. This is a case in which the Title VII and sec. 1981 claims "involve a common core of facts," and the theories cannot be viewed as a series of "discrete claims," Graham v. Sauk Prairie Police Commission, 915 F.2d 1085, 1109 (7th Cir. 1990). Therefore, the "fee award should not be reduced simply because the plaintiff failed to prevail on every contention raised in the lawsuit." Id.

Plaintiff's counsel is requested to prepare an appropriate judgment and to submit it to the court after first providing defendant's counsel with a copy.

Therefore, IT IS ORDERED that upon remand from the court of appeals for the seventh circuit, Mr. McKnight's claims under 42 U.S.C. sec. 1981 be and hereby are dismissed.

IT IS ALSO ORDERED that the defendant, General Motors', motion to limit the scope of reconsideration upon remand to the trial record be and hereby is granted.

IT IS FURTHER ORDERED that after reconsideration, Mr. McKnight's request for reinstatement to a position within the defendant corporation, General Motors, be and hereby is denied.

IT IS FURTHER ORDERED that Mr. McKnight's request for front pay in lieu of reinstatement be and hereby is denied.

IT IS FURTHER ORDERED that the defendant's motion to reduce the award of plaintiff's attorney's fees be and hereby is denied.

IT IS FURTHER ORDERED that each party shall bear its own costs in connection with this order on remand. No additional attorney's fees will be granted in connection with this order on remand.

Dated at Milwaukee, Wisconsin, this 15th day of July, 1991.

Myron L. Gordon
Senior U.S. District Judge

Appendix

Petition for a Writ of Certiorari

In The
Supreme Court of the United States

October, 1992 Term

No. _____

GARY McKNIGHT, Petitioner,

GENERAL MOTORS CORPORATION, Respondent.

PETITION FOR A WRIT OF CERTIORARI
TO THE UNITED STATES COURT OF APPEALS
FOR THE SEVENTH CIRCUIT

Gary McKnight
Pro SeIn TheSupreme Court of the United States

October, 1992 Term

No. _____

GARY McKNIGHT, Petitioner,

GENERAL MOTORS CORPORATION, Respondent

PETITION FOR A WRIT OF CERTIORARI
TO THE UNITED STATES COURT OF APPEALS

FOR THE SEVENTH CIRCUIT

The Petitioner, Gary McKnight, respectfully requests that a writ of certiorari issue to review the judgment and opinion of the United States Court of Appeals for the Seventh Circuit entered on September 11, 1992.

Questions Presented

I.   Whether the Court below's judicial decisions operate contrary to well-established United States Supreme Court holdings and that of the legislative intent of the United States Congress in regards to the relevant statutes and Senate Conference report H.R. 1746, 118 Congressional Record 7166, 7168 concerning section 706(g) thereof.

II. Whether the Court below's determinations not to provide the petitioner a Hearing on the matter of resolving remanded issues involving complex claims of entitlements of the relevant statutes of Title VII 42 U.S.C. 2000(e)-5, was contrary to that of sound judicial purpose.

III. Whether the Court below is permitted to deny established entitlements, that if provided would be consistent with the principle meaning of the relevant statute and judicial determinations of this court, to provide some restoration in the direction of "make whole" remedy of the provisions in regards to reinstatement, front pay in lieu of reinstatement or some other remedial form for the aggrieved.

IV. Whether the Court below should be allowed to operate in disregard to the reality and factual matters regarding actual damages and all forms of damages caused the aggrieved petitioner by the unlawful conduct of the respondent, and in direct conflict with constitutional principles.

V.   Whether the Court below either abused or misapplied its "broad discretion" regarding the denial of reinstatement or in lieu thereof front pay; and denying preinterest on the original judgment while the petitioner is saddled with inequity.

Table of Contents

Statement of the Case
Reasons for Granting

Table of Authorities

Cases:Page

Lemon v. Kurtzman, 411 U.S. 192, 201 (1973) (Opinion of C.J. Burger)

McKnight v. General Motors Corporation, 705 F.Supp. 464 (E.D. Wis. 1989)

McKnight v. General Motors Corporation, 908 F.2d 104, 105, 110-11 (7th Cir. 1990)

McKnight v. General Motors Corporation, 768 F.Supp. 675 (E.D. Wis. 1991)
McKnight v. General Motors Corporation, 973 F.2d 1366 (7th Cir. 1992)

McMullan v. Thornburg, 508 F.Supp. 1044 (E.D. Pa. 1981)

Miller v. Swisse Holding, Inc., (D.C. SNY 7/18/91) FEP Cases U.S.D.C. 1332

Patterson v. American Tobacco Co., 535 F.2d 257 12 FEP 314 (4th Cir. 1976)
Rios v. Enterprise Assn. Steamfitters Local 638 of UA, 501 F.2d 622 (1974)
Sampson v. Murray, 415 U.S. 61, 68, 90 (1974)

Shore v. Federal Express Corp., 777 F.2d 1155, 1159 (6th Cir. 1985)

Transworld Airlines v. Hardison, 432 U.S. 63, 82, 97 S. Ct. 2264, 14 FEP Cases 1697, 1977)

United States v. Georgia Power Co., U.S. Ct. App. 5th Cir. (New Orleans), 474 F.2d 906 (1973)

Wicker v. Hoppock, 6 Wall. 94, 99 (1897), the court goes on to state

Opinion Below

The opinion of the Court of Appeals affirms that of the District Court of the Eastern District of Wisconsin as to deny the Petitioner remanded entitlements involving reinstatement, in lieu thereof front pay and preinterest on the original Judgment awarded available under the relevant statute pursuant to Title VII.

Jurisdiction

The Judgment of the Court of Appeals for the Seventh Circuit was entered on September 11, 1992. This petition for certiorari was filed within 90 days of that date. This Court's jurisdiction is invoked under 28 U.S.C. sec. 1254(1). It is found in Article III, section II of the United States Constitution that the judicial power vested in the Supreme Court pursuant to Article III, section I apply to "all cases, in law and equity, arising under this constitution, the laws of the United States."

Statutory Provisions Involved

The provisions of Title VII of the Civil Rights Act of 1963, 42 U.S.C. sec. 2OOO(e)-5; and in part to the relevant subsections of the United States Senate

Conference report H.R. 1746, 118 Congressional Record 7166, 7168 concerning sec. 706(g) thereof as to the legislative purpose of the statute.

Statement of the Case

In October of 1988, the Petitioner, Gary McKnight prevailed on his claim in the District Court for the Eastern District of Wisconsin that the Defendant, General Motors Corporation, unlawfully terminated him from his employment in retaliation for filing complaints of race discrimination and because of his race. The Petitioner pursued his case under Title VII of the Civil Rights Act of 1964, 42 U.S.C. sec. 2OOO(e) et seq., and 42 U.S.C. sec. 1981, of the Civil Rights Act of 1866. The Petitioner's Title VII claims were to be resolved by the District Court pursuant to the operants of the relevant statutes and the 42 U.S.C. claims were determined by a jury in District Court. A Judgment was entered for the Petitioner, Gary McKnight, in the amount of $610,000.00, plus attorneys fees. More specifically, the jury awarded $55,000.00 in back pay, another $55,000.00 for emotional distress and $500,000.00 in punitive damages. The entitlements of reinstatement to the Petitioner's former position was denied on account of the Defendant's hostility, the trial court determined without evidentiary hearing that General Motors was hostile and the parties at best were acrimonious. The trial court further positioned itself for the denial of reinstatement on the foundation of the jury award, and said that reinstatement of the Petitioner, Gary McKnight, to his former position would not advance the purposes of the statute. The Petitioner, with full knowledge of the trial court judge's determination not to reinstate him on the grounds of the defendant, General Motors', hostility. Because General Motors is a tremendously large employer with a variety of relative positions to accommodate the Petitioner, Gary McKnight, McKnight provided a request for consideration of alternative positions of reinstatement in order to get his job back, along with the career he had lost, in order to get around what the trial judge determined as hostility of Defendant as a direct result of the unlawful conduct. The trial judge in the district court denied the Petitioner reinstatement further, McKnight v. General Motors Corporation, 705 F.Supp. 464 (E.D. Wis. 1989).

The Respondent, General Motors, appealed the judgment except for attorney's fees awarded to the plaintiff, and the Petitioner appealed his Title VII portion denying reinstatement and in lieu thereof front pay.

In June of 1989, this matter was pending on appeal, while at the same time the United States Supreme Court decided Patterson v. McLean Credit Union, 491 U.S. 164, 176 (1989) which pertains to sec. 1981 regarding the unlawful conduct of discrimination that occurs during the initial formation and making of contract; that is, that conduct which occurs during the initial hire of an employment relationship and not post-formative conduct as in regards to following the initial hire.

The Court of Appeals for the Seventh Circuit decided, during this matter's pending on appeal, that Patterson v. McLean Credit Union, 491 U.S. 164, 176 (1989) should be applied retroactively to obviate a substantial remedy provided to the Petitioner, McKnight. See McKnight v. General Motors Corporation, 908 F.2d 104, 110-11 (7th Cir. 1990). The Court of Appeals had determined that the Petitioner's sec. 1981 claims were not available and remanded to the District trial court below the matter of reinstatement on the grounds that the Defendant, General Motors, should not be allowed to benefit from its own hostility and that the size of the remaining judgment, a second consideration of the trial judge for his denying reinstatement in the first instance, had been substantially reduced. The matter of front pay if reinstatement was not practical, was also remanded to the Trial Judge for consideration. The Court of Appeals determined in the first instant that reinstatement is available under Petitioner's surviving entitlement under Title VII of the Civil Rights Act, 42 U.S.C. sec. 2000 etc.(e), McKnight v. General Motors Corporation, 908 F.2d 104, 110-11 (7th Cir. 1990).

On remand the District trial court held that the Petitioner, McKnight, is to be denied the only relief to "make whole" the Petitioner. See Albermarle Paper Co. v. Moody, (Nos. 74-389 and 74-428 10 FEP, 422 U.S. 405, 418-419 (1975). The District Court more specifically denied Mr. McKnight reinstatement to his former position or a neutral alternative position of the large employer, whose reservoir of positions are many, on the grounds of suggestion of the Petitioner, McKnight's, request to consider an alternative position if the trial judge continued denial of reinstatement to his former position because the Defendant was hostile. This obviated the Petitioner, McKnight's, career and offered him nothing in return. See McKnight v. General Motors Corporation, 768 F.Supp. 675 (E.D. Wis. 1991). The District Trial Court further denied the plaintiff (Petitioner) front pay in lieu thereof on the grounds that the jury did not establish loss of future earning capacity at the time of trial although testimony was offered that there was, in fact, a loss of future earnings capacity caused by the unlawful conduct of the Defendant, General Motors Corporation. The jury knew of the original judgment awarded the plaintiff and did not know that the trial judge did not reinstate the plaintiff (Petitioner) to his former position as the trial was held in 1988 and the reinstatement and front pay issues were decided after the verdict of the jury, before entry of judgment, and again decided by the trial court July 15, 1991. The Defendant, General Motors Corporation, in accordance with the relevant statute, posted a Supersedas Bond to satisfy statutory requirements concerning the original judgment and interest concerns thereof during the pendency of the appeal involving the original judgment. The Supersedas Bond was released on remand. A claim for what was left of the judgment ($55,000) asserted. The

Petitioner also asserted the matter of preinterest on what was left of the original judgment ($55,000). The Trial Court further denied preinterest on the judgment and did not consider any other form of remedy to "make whole" the Petitioner. See McKnight v. General Motors Corporation, 768 F.Supp. 675 (E.D. Wis. 1991); and Albermarle Paper Co. v. Moody, 422 U.S. 405 418-419 (1975).

The Petitioner, McKnight, appealed the issue of reinstatement, front pay in lieu of reinstatement and the matter regarding the issue of "preinterest". The defendant (Respondent), General Motors, cross-appealed the issue of attorney's fees and costs and did not make it available to the Petitioner during the pendency of that appeal to the Seventh Circuit for the remanded issues taken back up again.

On September 11, 1992, the U.S. Court of Appeals for the Seventh Circuit affirmed the decision of the District Court of the Eastern District of Wisconsin.

The U.S. Court of Appeals denied the Petitioner's claims to reinstatement and front pay on the testimony of the defense's own argument as to what the Petitioner, McKnight's career objectives are. This is speculative and highly prejudicial. The unlawful conduct as perpetrated by the defendant, General Motors, has resulted in occupational harm to the Petitioner and should be resolved accordingly, i.e., Sampson v. Murray, 415 U.S. 61, 68, 90 (1974). The U.S. Court of Appeals for the Seventh Circuit also denied the Petitioner appellant the in lieu thereof reinstatement "front pay" on the grounds that it is speculative and that "the longer a proposed front pay period, the more speculative the damages become," i.e., Hybert v. Hearst Corp., 900 F.2d 1050, 1056 (7th Cir. 1990). This is in conflict with the broad discretion so vested in the trial court to provide an equitable remedy to the plaintiff for his injuries.

In Sampson v. Murray, the United States Supreme Court commented that "in extraordinary cases irreparable injury might be found in discharge cases as to warrant preliminary injunctive relief," i.e., Sampson v. Murray, 415 U.S. at 96 415 U.S. 61 N68 (1974).

Reinstatement, in general, is the most favored form of equitable relief;, it is usually accompanied by an award of back pay. In McMullan v. Thornburgh, 508 F.Supp. 1044 (E.D. Pa 1981) the court held that "the unlawfully discharged employee had a superior claim to the position," and ordered reinstatement.

Chief Justice Rehnquist, in his opinion regarding the relevant issue here, determined the "thrust of sec. 703(h) of Title VII to be the authority to challenge, the failure to grant seniority or reinstatement is that of a discriminatory practice because it perpetuates the effects of pre-act discrimination, ante at 12."

The determination of the court below is in conflict with well-established holdings of many courts as to the matter involving reinstatement and front pay issues before it. See Davis v. San Francisco Municipal Ry, 11 FEP 1397, 1400

(N.D. Cal 1975); also, United States v. Navajo Freight Lines, Inc., 525 F.2d 1318, 1328, 11 FEP 787, 794 (9th Cir. 1975).

Courts have held opinions approving front pay. See Patterson v. American Tobacco Co., 535 F.2d 257, 12 FEP 314 (4th Cir. 1976); also Curtis v. Loether, 415 U.S. 189, 195 (1974). Id. 12 FEP at 323 N.10; Shore v. Federal Express Corp., 777 F.2d 1155, 1159 (6th Cir. 1985).

Reasons for Granting of Writ

I. The Decision Below Conflicts With Well-Established Judicial Holdings of Most Courts and Does Not Confer with the Intent of this Court.

The United States Supreme Court decided on June 25, 1975 in its holdings in Albermarle Paper Co. v. Moody, 422 U.S. 405, 418-419 (1975) that the objective here was to "make whole" the aggrieved party of unlawful discriminatory conduct. The court here also held that in instances the remedy of "back pay" alone is not sufficient to provide "make whole" relief. The fact here is that the Petitioner has not been made whole with his reduced remedy.

The United States Supreme Court also held in Sampson v. Murray, 415 U.S. 61 N68 at 96 (1974) that "in extraordinary cases irreparable injury might be found in discharge cases as to warrant preliminary injunctive relief." In fact, if one could fathom, General Motors' involvement here is an extraordinary case and, given its notoriety, the involvement alone could cause irreparable harm to the plaintiff.

In Miller v. Swisse Holding, Inc., (D.C. NY 7/18/91) 56 FEP Cases 1332, the District Court ordered reinstatement at salary comparable to what he would have achieved had he not been discharged.

The Supreme Court has clearly stated that "the unmistakable purpose of sec. 703(h) was to provide immunity for the operation. An application of a bona fide seniority system," see Transworld Airlines, Inc. v. Hardison, 432 U.S. 63, 82, 975 Ct. 2264, 14 FEP cases 1697.

Several circuit courts have attempted to move in the direction of providing the aggrieved individual with "make whole" remedy in keeping with the intent of sound judicial offering by either reinstating the unlawfully terminated employee or providing him other equitable forms of remedy in the form of "front pay." See Daniels v. Essex Group, Inc., (D.C. N. Ind 6/27/90) 53 FEP Cases 482, i.e. Deloach v. Delchamps, Inc., (CA5) 4/6/90 52 FEP Cases 1121.

It was proven in the case of McKnight v. General Motors, 973 F.2d 1366 (7th Cir. 1992) that a deliberate wrong of unlawful conduct had been perpetrated against the Petitioner and requires an adequate form of redress. "The general rule is that when a wrong has been done, and the law gives remedy, the compensation shall be equal to the injury. The injured party is to be placed as near as may be in the situation he would have occupied if the wrong had not been committed." Quoting Wicker v. Hoppock, 6 Wall. 94, 99 (1897), the court quoted:

> In the opinion of Chief Justice Burger, "In equity, as nowhere else, courts eschew rigid absolutes and look to the practical realities and necessities inescapably involved in reconciling competing interest." See Lemon v. Kurtzman, 411 U.S. 192, 201 (1973).

The court below did not conform to these holdings or reasons and is in conflict with the purpose and objectives therein.

These conflicts and judicial holdings provide some foundation as to justify the allowance certiorari to review the judgment below.

II. The Decision Below Provides Substantial Digression as to its Discretion as Not to Conform with the Trial Court's Vested Authority of Broad Discretion to Fully Restore and "Make Whole" the Aggrieved Under the Relevant Statute of Title VII of the Civil Rights Act of 1964, 42 U.S.C. sec. 2000(e) et seq. and that of Senate Conference Report H.R. 1746, 118 Congressional Record 7166, 7168 Concerning sec. 706(g).

It was Congress' intent in sec. 706(q)118 Congressional Record 7168 (1972) "to give the courts wide discretion to exercise their equitable powers to fashion the most complete relief possible. The expansive language of Section 706(g) and the 1972 legislative history support directives to the district courts to provide "make whole" relief liberally and not refuse it arbitrarily as to their determinations of redress for the aggrieved person. Discretion is vested to provide the most complete achievement and advancement of the objectives of Title VII that is attainable under the facts and circumstances of a particular case. The court below is not keeping with the objectives to provide "make whole" remedy.

Accordingly, the district court's denial of any form of seniority or relief must be reviewed in terms of the objectives of the statute. There is nothing in the statute that would draw a conclusion that Congress intended that statutory language ignored, or vest authority therein the trial court to wipe out the remedies available to the aggrieved person on a presumption created by the trial court contrary to the objectives of "making whole" that person.

To quote Chief Justice Burger, "Although retroactive benefit-type seniority relief may sometimes be appropriate and equitable, competitive-type seniority relief at the expense of wholly innocent employees can rarely, if ever, be equitable if that term retains traditional meaning. More equitable would be a monetary award to the person suffering the discrimination, an award such as 'front pay' could replace the need for competitive type seniority relief." See, ante, at 28 n.38.

In Franks v. Bowman Transportation Co., 495 F2d 398 (1974), U.S. Court of Appeals for the Fifth Circuit, the United States Supreme Court clearly indicated that the interests must bend to the overriding legislative policy in favor of "making whole" those who themselves were victims of the unlawful conduct thereof.

The court below conflicts with these clearly established objectives of the intent of the legislature. The court below also conflicts with other circuit courts. Quite clearly, the objective here does not advance the purpose of Title VII sec. 2OOOe.

The legislature has required reinstatement of an unlawfully discharged employee by an employer, when an employee has proven a violation of unlawful conduct or that of discrimination because of race, color, creed or sex. See Equal Employment Act of 1972, U.S.C. sec. 2000e-5(g)(1974), i.e. Ezekial v. Winkley, 20 Cal. 3d. 267, 142 Cal. Rptr. 418, 572, P.2d 32 (1977) won reinstatement for not being able to estimate money damages.

The eligible member should be placed back in the position which was his to enjoy had it not been for the unlawful conduct. See Rios v. Enterprise Assn. Steamfitters Local 638 of UA, 501 F.2d 622 (1974) U.S. Court of Appeals Second Circuit (New York).

Conclusion

For the aforementioned reasons, the allowance of certiorari to review the Judgment and Opinion of the Court below, of the Seventh Circuit.

Thank you for the consideration you have given this matter.

Respectfully submitted,

GARY McKNIGHT
Pro SeIn TheSupreme Court of the United States

APPENDIX A

UNITED STATES COURT OF APPEALS
FOR THE SEVENTH CIRCUIT

Nos. 89-1379, 89-1526

Date: July 2, 1990

BEFORE: Honorable Richard A. Posner, Circuit Judge
Honorable Frank H. Easterbrook, Circuit Judge
Honorable Thomas E. Fairchild, Senior Circuit Judge

GARY McKNIGHT,

Plaintiff-Appellee, Cross-Appellant
v.
GENERAL MOTORS CORPORATION,

Defendant-Appellant, Cross-Appellee.

Appeal from the United States District Court
for the Eastern District of Wisconsin.
No. 87 C 248—Judge Myron L. Gordon.

This cause was heard on the record from the above mentioned district court, and was argued by counsel.

On consideration whereof, IT IS ORDERED AND ADJUDGED by this Court that the judgment of the District Court in this cause appealed from be, and the same is hereby, AFFIRMED insofar as it awards McKnight back pay under Title VII, but otherwise REVERSED with directions to dismiss McKnight's section 1981 claims and REMANDED for reconsideration of his entitlement to reinstatement (or in lieu thereof to front pay) under Title VII. There shall be no award of costs in this Court and Circuit Rule 36 shall not apply on remand. These directions are in accordance with the opinion of this Court filed this date.

A true Copy:
Teste: _____

> Clerk of the United Staes Court of
> Appeals for the Seventh Circuit

Appendix B

Nos. 91-2989, 91-2990

GARY McKNIGHT,

Plaintiff-Appellant, Cross-Appellee,

v.

GENERAL MOTORS CORPORATION,

Defendant-Appellant, Cross-Appellee.

Appeal from the United States District Court
for the Eastern District of Wisconsin.
No. 87 C 248-Myron L. Gordon, Judge.

Argued June 8, 1992—Decided September 11, 1992

Before BAUER, Chief Judge, CUMMINGS, Circuit Judge, and FAIRCHILD, Senior Circuit Judge.

BAUER, Chief Judge. In this appeal, we review for the second time Gary McKnight's claim that he should be reinstated to his employment at General Motors Corporation ("GM"). We first reviewed his claim in 1990, after he won a jury verdict on a 42 U.S.C. sec. 1981 claim and a judgment under Title VII. McKnight v. General Motors Corp., 908 F.2d 104 (7th Cir. 1990) ("McKnight II"). On the sec. 1981 claim, the jury awarded McKnight $55,OOO in compensatory damages,

$55,000 in back pay, and $500,000 in punitive damages. The jury awarded no damages based on impairment of future earning capacity. On the Title VII claim tried before the court, the judge declined to order GM to reinstate McKnight. The only other relief McKnight requested under Title VII was back pay, which was rendered superfluous by the jury's $55,000 back pay award. McKnight v. General Motors Corp., 705 F.Supp. 464, 468 (E.D. Wis. 1989)("McKnight I").

We reversed the verdict under sec. 1981 in light of Patterson v. McLean Credit Union, 491 U.S. 164 (1989), and remanded those claims to the district court for dismissal. McKnight II, at 908 F.2d at 115, 117. We upheld the Title VII verdict, and affirmed McKnight's back pay award under that theory. We also directed the court to reconsider its refusal to reinstate McKnight and to determine, if reinstatement was not appropriate, whether McKnight should receive front pay in lieu of reinstatement. Id. We direct interested readers to McKnight I and II for the underlying facts in this case.

On remand, the district court reconsidered its reinstatement order, and again declined to order GM to reinstate McKnight or to award front pay. The court also denied McKnight's motion to reconsider that decision. Written opinions on both decisions were published in McKnight v. General Motors Corp., 768 F.Supp. 675 (E-D. Wis. 1991)("McKnight III"). McKnight appeals, arguing that the court abused its discretion in denying the relief he requests. He also contends that the court disobeyed our instructions in McKnight II on remand because it did not reopen the record and take evidence on McKnight's then-current financial condition, employment status, and his relationships with existing GM employees. McKnight also argues that he was entitled to prejudgment interest, and that the district court abused its discretion in refusing to award it. On cross-appeal, GM argues that the attorneys' fees award entered after trial pursuant to a stipulation by the parties should be reduced in light of our dismissal of McKnight's sec. 1981 claims. We shall discuss each claim in turn.

Reopening the Record

We do not believe the district court abused its discretion in declining to reopen the record or in refusing to order reinstatement or front pay. In its initial opinion, McKnight I, the district court stated that reinstatement was not appropriate in this case because the relationship between McKnight and GM was acrimonious, and because McKnight preferred not to be reinstated in his former position, but in a corporate finance or banking position. Reinstatement was also inappropriate, it found, because

It is clear that in the instant case the plaintiff has been fully compensated and thereby made whole by the award of compensatory damages, and the defendant has been properly punished by the award of punitive damages. Complete justice requires no more in the context of the remedial purpose of Title VII. 705 F.Supp. at 469. Based on this language, we found that "the district judge declined to order [reinstatement] because the relationship between McKnight and GM had been poisoned by this litigation and also because the award of $500,000 in punitive damages, on top of the compensatory damages awarded, was remedy enough." McKnight II, 908 F.2d at 115.

Because we struck the punitive and compensatory damages, we ordered the district court to reconsider its refusal to order McKnight's reinstatement, or in lieu thereof, to award front pay. Contrary to McKnight's present contention however, we did not order the court to reopen the record and gather new evidence on McKnight's employment status. Our opinion was silent as to whether the record should be supplemented. That decision, together with the decision on the merits, was left to the sound discretion of the trial judge. "A discretionary order will only be set aside if it is clear that no reasonable person could concur in the trial court's assessment." Tennes v. Commonwealth, 944 F.2d 372, 381 (7th Cir. 1991). "The district court's decision must strike us as fundamentally wrong for an abuse of discretion to occur." Anderson v. United Parcel Service, 915 F.2d 313, 315 (7th Cir. 1990).

The district judge declined to reopen the record for several reasons. He noted correctly that our opinion did not require it. McKnight III, 768 F.Supp. at 678. He also explained that Patterson did not alter the remedies available under Title VII. Finally, he noted that McKnight had a full opportunity at trial to present evidence of his past and future damages and had failed to provide any authority for his position that the district judge was required to reopen the record on remand.

McKnight's reliance on Grafenhain v. Pabst Brewing Co., 870 F.2d 1998, 1201 (7th Cir. 1989) and Welborn v. Reynolds Metals Co., 868 F.2d 389 (11th Cir. 1989), for the proposition that the district court was required to reopen the record because of our remand, is misplaced. A district court's duties on remand are governed by the opinion ordering it. As Black's dictionary defines it (and as we used the term in McKnight II), "reconsideration implies reexamination, and possibly a different decision by the entity that initially decided it." Black's Law Dictionary 1272 (6th ed. 1990). Although the district court in Grafenhain, reopened the record to determine the amount of front pay, as GM points out, it only did so after it determined based upon the trial record that front pay was appropriate. Id. at 1202. This is an important distinction—in Grafenhain, the amount of the award was determined in light of a reduction-in-force instituted by the defendant shortly after the plaintiff was wrongly discharged. Because the court found that the plaintiff would have lost his job for legitimate reasons during the RIF, it awarded front pay only for the period between the plaintiff's termination and the RIF. Id.

Similarly, in Welborn, the Eleventh Circuit reversed the district court's judgment that the plaintiff had failed to establish a prima facie case of discrimination. 810 F.2d 1026, 1028 (11th Cir. 1987). It remanded the case, and the district court reinstated the plaintiff but awarded back pay of only $1.00 because it found the plaintiff failed to present sufficient evidence at trial to support a larger award. The district court declined to receive additional evidence on back pay, either relating to the pre-trial or post-trial period. Welborn, 868 F.2d at 391. The Eleventh Circuit held that the district court could refuse to hear further evidence relating to the pre-trial period, but that it abused its discretion in refusing to hear evidence supporting a back-pay award from the time of trial until the plaintiff's reinstatement. Id. The court explained that there was no way for the plaintiff to present evidence at trial of her post-trial back-pay damages. Because Title VII is designed to make victims of discrimination whole, claimants are generally entitled to back pay from the date of the adverse employment action until reinstatement. Thus, the plaintiff should have been allowed to present evidence for the post-trial period. Id. at 391. The court also held that the plaintiff should have been allowed to present evidence on her reinstatement status. Id. But these rulings governed a proceeding where the appellate court reversed the trial court's judgment in favor of the defendant, and imposed liability. Because of its earlier judgment, the trial court in Welborn never evaluated the amount of back pay to which the plaintiff was entitled or to what position she should be reinstated. On remand, then, the court was required to evaluate what damages would make the plaintiff whole at the time the damages were awarded.

In this case, our remand was not based upon a reversal of the district court's evaluation of the facts at trial. Rather, because we vacated the sec. 1981 damages and questioned the completeness of the district court's explanation of its decision to deny reinstatement, we asked the district court to reconsider whether McKnight needed to be reinstated or given front pay to be made whole. This ruling did not require the district court to reopen the record, and we do not believe the court abused its discretion in refusing to do so.

Reinstatement Front Pay

As to the merits of the district court's refusal to reinstate McKnight, or to award front pay, we again note that this decision is consigned to the sound discretion of the district court. Tennes v. Commonwealth, 944 F.2d 372 (7th Cir. 1991);1 Grafenhain v. Pabst Brewing Co., 870 F.2d 1998, 1201 (7th Cir. 1989). "Under an abuse of discretion standard, the property inquiry is not how the reviewing court would have ruled if it had been considering the case in the first place, but rather whether any reasonable person could agree with the district court." Id. at 1201; see also EEOC v. Gurnee Inn Corp., 914 F.2d 815 (7th Cir. 1990).

Although reinstatement is usually the preferred remedy, reinstatement is not always required. The decision regarding reinstatement is within the discretion of the district court, and several factors may persuade the district judge after careful consideration in a particular case that the preferred remedy of reinstatement is not possible or is inappropriate.

Coston v. Plitt Theaters, Inc., 831 F.2d 1321, 1330 (7th Cir. 1987), cert. denied, 485 U.S. 1007, vacated on other grounds, 486 U.S. 1020, on remand, 860 F.2d 834 (7th Cir. 1988). In Coston, the two factors relied upon by the district court were hostility which it believed made reinstatement futile, and the lack of an available position for plaintiff. 831 F.2d at 1330. We also noted that genuine employer dissatisfaction with an employee's job performance is another factor for a court to consider in its determination whether reinstatement is apropriate. Id. at 1332. Nevertheless, we stated that we are "cognizant of the legitimate concern that the hostility common to litigation not become an excuse to avoid ordering reinstatement on a general basis . . . ." Id. at 1330. In Tennes, we affirmed the court's refusal to reinstate because we found the district court's determination that "there is no reason to believe the parties would enjoy a productive and amicable working relationship," and that the plaintiff "would not enjoy the confidence or respect of current management" was reasonable. Tennes, 944 F.2d at 381. The district court also declined to award front pay in part because the amount would be "too speculative" due to a high turn-over rate for other employees and because of the plaintiff's weak employment history in general and with the employer in particular. Id.

The jury refused to award McKnight damages for "loss of future earning capacity" caused by GM's discrimination. See Special Verdict at 2, Rec. Doc. 83. A jury's verdict, when sec. 1981 and Title VII claims are tried simultaneously, binds the judge on factual issues common to both claims. Daniels v. Pipefitters Association, 945 F.2d 906, 923 (7th Cir. 1991) (citing cases), cert. denied, 112 S.Ct. 1514 (1992). Therefore, we believe the trial judge was bound by the jury's determination that McKnight suffered no impairment of his future earning ability. Damages for impaired future earning capacity are generally awarded in tort suits when a plaintiff's physical injuries diminish his earning power. See, e.g., Johnson v. Director, 911 F.2d 247 (9th Cir. 1990) (worker's compensation), cert. denied sub nom., Todd Pacific Shipyards Corp. v. Director, 111 S.Ct. 1582 (1991); Gorniak v. National Railroad Passenger Corp., 889 F.2d 481 (3d Cir. 1989) (FELA suit by railroad employee). We have also affirmed loss of earning capacity awards in employment discrimination cases. See Morales v. Cadena, 825 F.2d 1095, 1100 (7th Cir. 1987) (affirming award based on jury's consideration of plaintiff's emotional turmoil, depression, and career disruption). To recover for lost earning capacity, a plaintiff must produce "competent evidence suggesting that his injuries have narrowed the range of economic opportunities available to him . . . . [A] plaintiff must show that his injury has caused a diminution in his ability to earn a living." Gorniak, 889 F.2d at 484. Thus, the jury determined that McKnight's ability to earn from the time of trial onward was not impaired.

The trial court held that reinstatement was not apropriate because McKnight asked for a "completely different job and to be relocated in a new city." McKnight III, 768 F.Supp. at 679. The court found no basis to conclude that McKnight is qualified to perform the job he requests or that there is a position available. Id. at 680. Moreover, because McKnight's career goals have changed, the district court did not believe Title VII's purposes would be served by putting McKnight in a job "he does not want." Id. McKnight challenges this factual finding, and argues that the court should have considered his present "desperate" financial condition. The court noted the possibility that McKnight requests reinstatement to force GM to buy him out. As we pointed out, such motivation is a valid reason for denial. McKnight II, 908 F.2d at 116. Finally, the court stated that the compensatory and punitive awards did not influence his initial decision not to reinstate McKnight given the change in career goals McKnight presented at trial. The court also repeated his concerns about the acrimonious relationship between the parties. Id. We cannot find that the district court abused its direction in basing its refusal to reinstate McKnight on these factors.

McKnight relies on Ellis v. Ringold School District, 832 F.2d 27 (3d Cir. 1987), cert. denied, 494 U.S. 1005 (1990), to challenge one of the district court's reasons for declining to reinstate him. At trial, McKnight presented extensive evidence that after his discharge, he changed his career and became a stockbroker. McKnight I, 705 F. Supp. at 469. Moreover, in his post-trial motion for reinstatement, McKnight stated that he preferred to be reinstated to a position as a corporate finance portfolio manager or analyst in GM's New York office. See Plaintiff's Reply Brief in Support of his Post-Verdict Motion for Reinstatement, Rec. Doc. 92, at 3-4. As we have noted, when the district court reconsidered McKnight's reinstatement, it relied in part upon this career change to refuse to reinstate McKnight to his position as a manufacturing supervisor. McKnight III, 768 F.Supp. at 680. The court also expressed concern over McKnight's ability to assume a position managing GM's corporate finances. Id.

In Ellis, after her discharge the plaintiff, a school teacher, worked for higher pay in a munitions factory for two years, then taught for a semester at a private school, and finally took a job as a janitor. 832 F.2d at 29. The district court did not discuss the plaintiff's request for reinstatement in its order, and the defendant argued on appeal that the plaintiff's decision to work in industry meant that she was not entitled to reinstatement as a teacher. Id. at 30. The Third Circuit noted that this "argument would have greater force if, in fact, the court had denied reinstatement." Id. Moreover, the court explained that "[s]tanding alone, the fact that a plaintiff takes a job in an unrelated field to meet her obligation of mitigation should not be construed as a voluntary withdrawal from her former profession." Id. The plaintiff asked to be reinstated to her former position as a teacher, which distinguishes her from the situation in the case at bar.

Further, in this case, the district court did consider and deny McKnight's request for reinstatement, and McKnight did more than take a job in an unrelated field. He testified at trial that he had become a stockbroker, and in his post-trial pleadings requesting reinstatement, expressed a preference for a job in his new field. The district court denied front pay on remand in part because the jobs McKnight held after his discharge from GM paid more. See 768 F.Supp. at 680; see also discussion of McKnight's post-GM employment history, infra at 10.

Damages in employment discrimination cases are not intended to insure a plaintiff's future financial success. "Damages should ordinarily extend only to the date upon which 'the sting' of any discriminatory conduct has ended." Smith v. Great American Restaurants, Inc., Nos. 91-1793 & 19-1864, 1992 U.S. App. LEXIS 16821, at 823 (7th Cir. July 24, 1992) (quoting Syvock v. Milwaukee Boiler Manufacturing Co., Inc., 665 F.2d 149, 160 n.14 (7th Cir. 1981). In fact, in Syvock, we approved the district court's determination that

> A proper cutoff time for a damage assessment in this case should be the day when the wounds of discrimination should have healed. In this case it is certain that the sting of any discriminatory conduct ended, or should have ended, substantially in advance of the date the trial on damages commenced.

665 F.2d at 160 n.14. McKnight presented himself to the jury as a successful stockbroker, and at the time of trial he was employed as a broker by Gruntol Corporation. Gruntol paid McKnight $12,840 in wages between April and August 1988. See Trial Transcript ("Tr. Trans."), Vol. IV-B at 48-49. McKnight kept this job until December of 1988. Affidavit of Gary McKnight, Rec. Doc. 146, at 1. Before he worked for Gruntol, McKnight told the jury that he worked as a broker for another company, Oppenheimer & Co., for approximately a year and a half. He earned about $54,000 from Oppenheimer in 1987. Tr. Trans. Vol. IV-B at 41. While he worked at GM, McKnight earned $32,000 a year. McKnight I, 708 F. Supp. at 468.

Based on this evidence, the court could have found that the sting of discrimination had ended by the time of trial. In any event, the jury did find that McKnight's future earning ability was not impaired. The district court also looked to this evidence when it denied reinstatement and front pay. He explained that "it is arguable that Mr. McKnight presented a 'success' story to the jury—electing to impress the jurors with his entitlement to large damages, both compensatory and punitive. He now would reverse his field and seek to demonstrate his impoverished condition at a reopened trial." McKnight III, 768 F.Supp. at 682. Here, through reinstatement or a front pay award, McKnight appears to be attempting to force GM to insure his future employment success. At trial he presented evidence that he had made a successful career change. Now, he presents evidence that he has had trouble keeping jobs since then. McKnight Affidavit, Rec. Doc. 146, at 1-2. Nevertheless, as we have explained, "you cannot just leave the labor force after being wrongfully discharged, in the hope of someday being made by a judgment at law." Hunter v. Allis-Chalmers Corp., 797 F.2d 1417, 1426 (7th Cir. 1986). McKnight's plea for help from his "desperate" financial decision does make us question whether he expects GM to ensure his future employment success. See Brief in Support of Plaintiff's Motion for Reconsideration, Rec. Doc. 145, and McKnight Affidavit, Rec. Doc. 146.

We also note that when a party fails to provide the district court with the essential data necessary to calculate a reasonably certain front pay award, the court may deny the front pay request. Coston, 831 F.2d at 1335, n.6. Such information includes the amount of the proposed award, the length of time the plaintiff expects to work for the defendant, and the applicable discount rate. Id. Moreover, front pay awards, while often speculative, cannot be unduly so. The longer a proposed front pay period, the more speculative the damages become. Hybert v. Hearst Corp., 900 F.2d 1050, 1056 (7th Cir. 1990). Here, McKnight provides no basis for calculating an appropriate award, even for the picture of his employment history he presented at trial. The district court invited the parties to file written memoranda further addressing the issues of reinstatement and front pay at a status conference held shortly after our remand. See May 16, 1991 Transcript at 4-5. Both parties declined. McKnight's motion for reconsideration also lacks the data the district court needed to calculate front pay.

Given the speculative nature of front pay in this case, together with McKnight's trial strategy and post-discharge employment history, we do not believe the district court abused its discretion in declining to order his reinstatement or to award front pay.

Prejudgment Interest

McKnight also challenges the district court's refusal to order GM to pay prejudgment interest on his back pay award. "An award of prejudgment interest lies within the discretion of the trial court." Kossman v. Calumet County, 800 F.2d 697, 702 (7th Cir. 1986), cert. denied, 479 U.S. 1088 (1987), appeal after remand, 849 F.2d 1027 (1988). In more recent cases, we have cabined that discretion somewhat. "The time has come, we think, to generalize, and to announce a rule that prejudgment interest should be presumptively available to victims of federal law violations." Gorenstein Enterprises v. Quality Care-USA, 874 F.2d 431, 436 (7th Cir. 1989). "Title VII authorizes prejudgment interest as part of the back pay remedy in suits against private employers." Loeffler v. Frank, 486 U.S. 549, 557 (1988). "Indeed, the Supreme Court has said that it is a `normal incident' of relief in Title VII suits." EEOC v. Gurnee Inn Corp., 914 F.2d 815, 819 (7th Cir. 1990) (quoting Loeffler, 486 U.S. at 558). Nevertheless, in Brooms v. Regal Tube Co., 881 F.2d 412 (7th Cir. 1989), we refused to grant a plaintiff's request for prejudgment interest because the plaintiff never presented the issue to the district court and raised it for the first time on appeal. We held that "at a minimum, a party must request the interest in a post-trial motion if he or she has failed to plead the relief in the original complaint." Brooms, 881 F.2d at 424 n.9 (citing Williamson v. Handy Button Machine Co., 817 F.2d 1290, 1298 (7th Cir. 1987).

Here McKnight did not ask for prejudgment interest until after we remanded the case and the district court entered its decision and order on remand on July 15, 1991. See Plaintiff's Motion for Order Requiring Payment of Partial Post-Judgment Interest and Pre-Judgment Interest, dated August 1, 1991, Rec. Doc. 147. This request came almost three years after the district court entered its first judgment, and much later than the plaintiff's request in Brooms. McKnight provides no explanation for his tardy motion. This case is clearly distinguishable from Williamson v. Handy Button Machine Co., 817 F.2d 1290, 1298 (7th Cir. 1987), where the plaintiff only waited until after the judgment was entered to ask for prejudgment interest. Here, McKnight waited through the district court's first entry of judgment, the appeal to his court, the remand, and entry of a second judgment before asking for interest. This is simply too long. Brooms, 881 F.2d at 424. Therefore, we find that the district court correctly denied as untimely McKnight's request for prejudgment interest.

Attorney's Fees

GM asks us to set aside the attorneys' fees award entered by the district court. The parties stipulated to the amount of fees prior to the first appeal in this case, and the district court's judgment is based on this stipulation. The district court was entitled to hold GM to the stipulation, absent "manifest injustice" to the parties. See Grafenhaim, 870 F.2d at 1206; see also Cates v. Morgan Portable Building Corp., 780 F.2d 683, 690-91 (7th Cir. 1985) ("Although stipulations are to be encouraged in order to economize on the costs of litigation, a judge has the power to relieve a party from a stipulation when it is reasonable to do so . . ."). The stipulation contemplated the possibility that the judgment might be modified on appeal. See Stipulation Regarding Attorneys' Fees, Rec. Doc. 104, at 2. Moreover, GM is a sophisticated litigant, and was represented by experienced counsel during the negotiation and entry of the stipulation. We do not believe the district court abused its discretion when it refused to relieve GM of the stipulation. Moreover, the district court determined that the fee award was "entirely reasonable" because the Title VII and sec. 1981 claims involved common facts. McKnight III, 768 F.Supp. at 681. Although we have ordered courts to reduce attorneys' fees awards in cases where sec. 1981 awards have been vacated, Brooms, 881 F.2d at 412; Coston v. Plitt Theaters, Inc., 860 F.2d 834 (7th Cir. 1988), appellate review of an attorneys' fees award is very limited. Kossman v. Calumet County, 849 F.2d 1027, 1030 (7th Cir. 1988). The district court's holding falls within its sound discretion, and we decline to disturb it.

For the foregoing reasons, the judgment of the district court is

AFFIRMED.

A true Copy:
Teste:

_____

Clerk of the United States Court of
Appeals for the Seventh Circuit

Appendix C

UNITED STATES DISTRICT COURT
EASTERN DISTRICT OF WISCONSIN

GARY McKNIGHT,

Plaintiff,

v.Case No. 87-C-248

GENERAL MOTORS CORPORATION,

Defendant.

DECISION AND ORDER ON REMAND

In 1988, Gary McKnight prevailed on his claim that the defendant, General Motors Corporation, unlawfully discharged him from his employment because of his race and in retaliation for his prior complaints of race discrimination. Mr. McKnight pressed his case under Title VII of the Civil Rights Act of 1964, 42 U.S.C. sec. 2000e et seq., and 42 U.S.C. sec. 1981, which is based on the Civil Rights Act of 1866. A jury heard his sec. 1981 claim, and this court resolved the Title VII dispute.

Judgment was entered in the plaintiff's favor in the amount of $610,000.00, plus attorney's fees. Specifically, the jury awarded $55,000.00 in back pay, another $55,000.00 for emotional distress, and $500,000.00 as punitive damages.

This court denied Mr. McKnight's post-trial motion for reinstatement to his former position as a manufacturing supervisor and his alternative request for reinstatement to a different job in a different location but still within the General Motors Corporation. McKnight v. General Motors Corp., 705 F.Supp. 464 (E.D. Wis. 1989). The defendant appealed the judgment except for the award of attorney's fees, and the plaintiff appealed that portion of the judgment denying reinstatement.

During the pendency of the appeal, the United States Supreme Court decided Patterson v. McLean Credit Union, 491 U.S. 164, 176 (1989), which holds that sec. 1981 was limited to providing redress for unlawful discrimination in the "making and enforcement of private contracts," and specifically held that sec. 1981 afforded no relief from "problems that may arise later from the conditions of continuing employment."

On appeal, the court of appeals for the seventh circuit decided that Patterson should be applied retroactively. McKnight v. General Motors Corp., 908 F.2d 104, 110-11 (7th Cir. 1990). The court of appeals directed me to dismiss Mr. McKnight's sec. 1981 claims. The court also remanded "for reconsideration of his entitlement to reinstatement (or in lieu thereof to front pay) under Title VII." Id. at 117.

The first issue raised here by the parties is the scope of consideration on remand. The defendant urges that the reconsideration is limited to the record as it stands; the plaintiff argues that the court should reopen the record to receive additional evidentiary submissions on the questions of reinstatement and front pay.

The instructions from the court of appeals do not expressly or impliedly call for additional evidence. The court's instructions are "to reexamine the issue of reinstatement in light of [the vacation of the punitive damage award] and also in light of our discussion in the preceding paragraph of the circumstances in which denial of reinstatement is appropriate." McKnight, 908 F.2d at 116. The court also stated that "on remand the district court may wish to consider not only whether McKnight should be reinstated but also whether, if not, he can and should receive front pay in lieu of reinstatement." Id. at 117.

Mr. McKnight argues that the change in the law occasioned by the Patterson decision had "obvious corresponding impacts on matters litigated in this case." Plaintiff's brief in opposition at p. 2. Patterson in no way changed the remedies available under Title VII. Reinstatement and front pay were available when the case was tried and still remain possible remedies under Title VII. I also reject the plaintiff's contention that his current employment situation must be explored in order to resolve the remanded matters. The record was fully established as of the end of the trial, unless there exists a contrary instruction from the appellate court. I cannot find such an instruction in the court of appeals' ruling. Mr. McKnight made his record regarding damages, both past and future, during the trial, and he submitted his case regarding reinstatement in post-trial briefs.

A status conference was held in open court on May 16, 1991. At that time, I heard the parties' positions as to the remanded issues and inquired of the parties whether they wanted to file written memoranda further addressing the issues of reinstatement and front pay. Surprisingly, both sides declined. The defendant did ask for and did receive an opportunity to brief the issue of attorneys' fees. The briefs on that one issue have been filed, and the issues remanded by the court of appeals are now ripe for review.

With reference to "the record" in this case, I am constrained to observe that the court of appeals addressed a matter of "trial error" that it acknowledged was not a part of the record. Indeed, it was a matter that the court of appeals expressly recognized was not preserved for appeal and had been waived. Nevertheless, the panel concluded that because of the time limitations which I set, the defendant's witnesses actually "ran" to and from the witness stand. This, the court of appeals stated, created a "spectacle" and a "relay race." It was "unseemly," the court of appeals went on to note. McKnight, 908 F.2d at 115.

Unfortunately, in going dehors the record, the court of appeals unfairly relied on the partisan representation of General Motors' disappointed trial counsel, whose prized client had suffered an adverse jury verdict of over $600,000. The appellate court's reliance was enhanced because Mr. McKnight's counsel understandably did not contradict the representation. Why, I ask, should plaintiff's counsel expend his valuable, restricted time to respond to an issue that was not preserved for appeal? He had to address other issues—ones based on the record—before his red light went on.

I have been a judge of a court of record for 40 years. In no instance, including the McKnight case, has a witness ever entered my courtroom on the run or exited from the witness stand at such a pace in a matter over which I have presided. The "unseemly spectacle" described in Judge Posner's decision simply did not take place. There was no "relay race." The court of appeals also asserted that my time limits were imposed "arbitrarily." My decision to set time limitations stemmed from the following circumstances: On March 5, 1987, this case was filed and was assigned to Judge Thomas J. Curran; he entered a scheduling order on July 20, 1987, in which he stated that the time necessary for trial was "a maximum of three days." Subsequently, the case was randomly reassigned to Judge J.P. Stadtmueller. When I then volunteered to handle it in place of Judge Stadtmueller, the case was about a year and a half old and, on its face, it was an uncomplicated employment discrimination case which should be tried in a maximum of three days.

I conducted a pretrial conference on August 8, 1988, and set the trial to start on October 3, 1988. However, as the two sides geared up for trial, I found that they were crossing swords at every turn. Representing General Motors, the defense team was playing hardball; Mr. McKnight's counsel was equally out for blood. During the rather short period between the pretrial conference and the start of the trial, the volume of filings in this case more than doubled. General Motors submitted an inordinately large number of in limine motions seeking to exclude testimony from various witnesses. For instance, in reference to the deposition of one witness alone, Jacob Johnson, the defendant asked me to resolve over 65 evidentiary objections in advance of trial. Five days before the trial date, the defendant filed a motion for reconsideration of Judge Curran's denial of its motion for summary judgment. His decision on the original motion had been entered on May 12, 1988.

Being unable to agree on the questions to be included in a special verdict, counsel filed widely divergent proposals. They also vigorously disagreed on their proposed substantive jury instructions and submitted separate ones. There were 105 exhibits to be offered in evidence, and pretrial objections were advanced as to most of them.

As the trial date neared, I became increasingly aware of the extraordinary combativeness of counsel. I was firmly convinced that they were turning an acorn into an oak tree right before my eyes. It was my studied opinion that this case could fairly be tried in one week; it would needlessly have taken far longer than that if counsel had a free rein. After discussing this problem with counsel, I set the time limits. No objections were heard. The time limitations were calmly and deliberately set to meet a clearly demonstrated need; they were not "arbitrarily" imposed. I was fully mindful of the admonitions in Flaminio v. Honda Motor Co., Ltd., 733 F.2d 463 (1964) in setting the time restrictions in advance of the trial and in keeping them flexible as the trial progressed. It is regrettable that the court of appeals elected to buy the version of how this trial was conducted that was sold by General Motors' lawyer. With that said, I turn to the issues at hand.

I. Reinstatement

The Title VII remedies in a particular case are to be fashioned in such a way as to return the victim of discrimination to the position he would have been in but for the illegal behavior. Albermarle Paper Co. v. Moody, 422 U.S. 405, 418-19 (1975). Reinstatement is not a tool to be used by an individual to fulfill his, as yet, unmet employment goals.

The court is to exercise its discretion so as to remedy the discrimination suffered by Mr. McKnight. One such potential remedy is reinstating Mr. McKnight to his former position. This remedy is in keeping with Albermarle. However, the remedy sought by Mr. McKnight is to be placed within General Motors in an entirely different job and to be relocated to a new city; that is his clear preference.

"A hiring order is not appropriate unless the person discriminated against is presently qualified to assume the position sought." Kamberos v. GTE Automatic Electric, Inc., 603 F.2d 598, 603 (7th Cir. 1979) (citing Franks v. Bowman Transportation Co., Inc., 424 U.S. 747 (1976)). Likewise, reinstatement is not warranted where the position sought is no longer available. Gaddy v. Abex Corp., 884 F.2d 312, 319 (7th Cir. 1989). The case at bar does not involve a discriminatory failure to hire or a discriminatory firing disguised as an elimination of position or a reduction in force. However, the underlying policy is still the same: reinstatement must be feasible. There is no basis to find that Mr. McKnight is presently qualified to assume his preferred position in "corporate finance or investment banking" or that General Motors has such a position available.

The court of appeals' decision surmised that the plaintiff's desire to be reinstated might be motivated by his wish to be bought out. McKnight, 980 F.2d at 116. This is not beyond the realm of possibility, especially in light of Mr. McKnight's changed career goals. Given Mr. McKnight's unequivocal desire to be in an entirely different field, reinstatement to his former position is not desirable or realistic.

Mr. McKnight could be reinstated to his former position as a manufacturing supervisor. Would the purposes of Title VII be advanced by such an order? I think not. Mr. McKnight's career goals and aspirations, as presented by his testimony at trial and through his experts, no longer include supervising the manufacture of automobile parts. He wants to be in the financial services industry. Title VII would not be served by placing the plaintiff in a job he does not want. Such a situation would likely cause Mr. McKnight to suffer again from emotional distress. This type of reaction "would ensue independently of any hostility or retaliation by the employer." Id.

I am directed to reexamine the issue of reinstatement in light of the fact that the punitive damage award and the compensatory damage award have been vacated. I do not believe that those circumstances change the equation. As stated in the original decision, a primary consideration in denying reinstatement was Mr. McKnight's express desire to work in another field. In ruling on the motions after judgment, I stated in the opinion published at 705 F.Supp. at 469:

> After balancing all the equities, I am convinced that reinstatement in this case would not advance the purposes of Title VII. The plaintiff asserts that he prefers not to be reinstated in his former position of manufacturing supervisor but rather in a position concerned with corporate finance or investment banking. Further, the evidence at trial established that the plaintiff has changed his career goal from manufacturing management to being a stockbroker. I conclude that the plaintiff does not have a primary interest in the position that he formerly held.

That aspect of the case has not been altered by my reconsideration of the issue on this remand. The matters of compensatory and punitive damages awarded for his sec. 1981 claim, as well as the "acrimonious" employer-employee relationship, were viewed as lesser considerations; I still view them as such.

II. Front Pay

Is front pay an available remedy under Title VII? Yes. Weaver v. Casa Gallardo, Inc., 922 F.2d 1515, 1528 (11th Cir. 1991); Carter v. Sedgwick County, Kansas, 929 F.2d 1501, 1505 (10th Cir. 1991); Edwards v. Occidental Chemical Corp., 892 F.2d 1442, 1449 (9th Cir. 1990); Shore v. Federal Express Corp., 777 F.2d 1155, 1159 (6th Cir. 1985). This list, while certainly not exhaustive, is representative of the jurisdictions which hold that front pay is available under Title VII when reinstatement is denied.

Is an award of front pay appropriate in the case at bar? No. Mr. McKnight presented evidence to the jury regarding his employment future. The jury reasonably found that Mr. McKnight did not lose future earnings as a result of the discrimination he suffered at the hands of the defendant. Mr. McKnight earned considerably more money after his termination from General Motors. I am persuaded that Mr. McKnight's employment opportunities were not and are not inferior to his employment at General Motors.

III. Attorney's Fees

After the resolution of the post-trial motions, but before the issuance of the appellate mandate, the parties entered into a stipulation regarding the plaintiff's attorney's fees and costs. Pursuant to that stipulation, this court entered an order amending the judgment to add an award of $57,125.70 as attorney's fees and costs. Although the defendant did not appeal this aspect of the judgment, it now seeks to have the attorney's fee award reduced.

I do not consider it appropriate to revisit the attorney's fees award. The United States Supreme Court has stated:

> When a case has been once decided by this court on appeal, and remanded to the Circuit Court, whatever was before this court, and disposed of by its decree, is considered as finally settled. The Circuit Court is bound by the decree as the law of the case, and must carry it into execution, according to the mandate. That court cannot vary it, or examine it for any other purpose than execution; or give any other or further relief; or review it, even for apparent error, upon any matter decided on appeal; or intermeddle with it, further than to settle so much as has been remanded.

In re Sanford Fork & Tool Co., 160 U.S. 247, 255 (1895).

A lower court may decide matters left open by the mandate. Id. However, the issue of attorney's fees was not left open by the mandate of the court of appeals. How could it have been left open when the issue was not raised on appeal?

Even if I revisited the issue of attorney's fees, I would not disturb the stipulation previously entered by the parties. The amount of attorney's fees and costs was entirely reasonable. This is a case in which the Title VII and sec. 1981 claims "involve a common core of facts," and the theories cannot be viewed as a series of "discrete claims." Graham v. Sauk Prairie Police Commission, 915 F.2d 1085, 1109 (7th Cir. 1990). Therefore, the "fee award should not be reduced simply because the plaintiff failed to prevail on every contention raised in the lawsuit." Id.

Plaintiff's counsel is requested to prepare an appropriate judgment and to submit it to the court after first providing defendant's counsel with a copy.

Therefore, IT IS ORDERED that upon remand from the court of appeals for the seventh circuit, Mr. McKnight's claims under 42 U.S.C. sec. 1981 be and hereby are dismissed.

IT IS ALSO ORDERED that the defendant, General Motors', motion to limit the scope of reconsideration upon remand to the trial record be and hereby is granted.

IT IS FURTHER ORDERED that after reconsideration, Mr. McKnight's request for reinstatement to a position within the defendant corporation, General Motors, be and hereby is denied.

IT IS FURTHER ORDERED that Mr. McKnight's request for front pay in lieu of reinstatement be and hereby is denied.

IT IS FURTHER ORDERED that the defendant's motion to reduce the award of plaintiff's attorney's fees be and hereby is denied.

IT IS FURTHER ORDERED that each party shall bear its own costs in connection with this order on remand. No additional attorney's fees will be granted in connection with this order on remand.

Dated at Milwaukee, Wisconsin, this day of July, 1991.

_____

Senior U.S. District Judge

APPENDIX D

UNITED STATES DISTRICT COURT
EASTERN DISTRICT OF WISCONSIN

GARY McKNIGHT,

Plaintiff,

v.Case No. 87-C-0248

GENERAL MOTORS CORPORATION,

Defendant.

DECISION AND ORDER

Commencing on October 3, 1988, a jury trial was held on the plaintiff's claims, pursuant to 42 U.S.C. sec. 1981 and Title VII, that the defendant unlawfully discharged him from his employment at A. C. Sparkplug because of his race and in retaliation for his prior complaints of race discrimination. The jury returned a verdict in favor of the plaintiff on both the discrimination claim and the retaliation claim. The jury awarded $110,000 in compensatory damages and $500,000 in punitive damages.

The defendant has now filed motions after verdict seeking: (a) a judgment notwithstanding the verdict; or in the alternative, (b) an order amending the judgment to strike the award of punitive damages and reduce the amount of the compensatory damages; and (c) a new trial on various grounds. The plaintiff has filed a post verdict motion to amend the judgment to provide for his reinstatement to his prior job or to a comparable position. For reasons stated herein, the defendant's several motions will be denied, as will the plaintiff's motion for reinstatement.

Motions for a judgment notwithstanding the verdict are to be weighed by the following legal standard:

> Such a motion should be denied "where the evidence, along with inferences to be reasonably drawn therefrom, when viewed in the light most favorable to the party opposing such motion, is such that reasonable men in a fair and impartial exercise of their judgment may reach different conclusions." Smith v. J. C. Penney Company, 7 Cir., 1958, 261 F.d2 218, 219.

Rakovich v. Wade, No.85-1529 and 85-1530, slip op. at 12 (7th Cir. June 8, 1988) (en banc) (quoting Valdes v. Karoll's, Inc., 277 F.2d 637, 638 (7th Cir. 1960).

In deciding whether the evidence is sufficient to satisfy this standard, the district court is not to weigh the evidence or judge the credibility of the witnesses nor substitute its own judgment of the facts for that of the jury. Rakovich, supra, at 12-13. The district court, however, should consider whether the evidence to support the verdict is substantial; "a mere scintilla of evidence will not suffice." La Montagne v. American Convenience Products, Inc., 750 F.2d 1405, 1410 (7th Cir. 1984).

I find that there was ample credible evidence to support the jury's findings that the defendant discriminated against the plaintiff on the basis of his race, and also, that it retaliated against him for having filed complaints alleging race discrimination. Similarly, there was sufficient evidence to warrant the jury's finding that the defendant took these actions in a malicious, wanton or oppressive manner.

The order of proof in a case such as this is set forth in McDonnell Douglas Corp. v. Green, 411 U.S. 792, 802 (1973), and in Texas Dept. of Community Affairs v. Burdine, 450 U.S. 248, 254 (1980). Under the prescribed model of proof, the plaintiff must first establish a prima facie case. To do this the plaintiff must (1) prove that he is a member of a protected class, (2) prove that he was discharged, and (3) produce sufficient evidence of disparate treatment that the court can infer a causal connection between his protected class membership and the discharge. Similarly, in order to establish a prima facie case of retaliation, the plaintiff must show that: "(1) he has engaged in statutorily protected activity; (2) that the employer has taken adverse employment action; and (3) a causal connection exists between the two." Donnellon v. Fruehauf Corp., 794 F.2d 598, 600 (11th Cir. 1986).

The prima facie case serves the function of eliminating the most common non-discriminatory reasons for the employer's adverse action against the plaintiff, giving rise to a legally mandatory presumption of intent to discriminate on a prohibited basis. Burdine, supra, 450 U.S. at 254 n.7. The burden then shifts to the employer to rebut the presumption by articulating a legitimate, nondiscriminatory reason for the discharge. Id. The burden then shifts back to the plaintiff to prove that the articulated reason is pretextual. This may be accomplished directly by persuading the trier of fact "that a discriminatory reason more likely motivated the employer or indirectly by showing that the employer's proffered explanation is unworthy of credence." Burdine, supra, 450 U.S. at 256. If the articulated reason is shown to be pretextual, then the initial presumption is in effect resurrected and stands unrebutted.

In McDonnell Douglas, the Supreme Court held that in an individual race discrimination case, the employee may focus on employment patterns broader than his own individual case to prove pretext. Id. at 804-05. An employer's deviation from normal patterns and practices, the subjectivity of the employment evaluation system relied upon by the employer and the racial attitudes of the supervisors in question are generally considered relevant in this regard. Id.; Hunter v. Allis-Chalmers Corp., 797 F.2d 1417, 1423 (7th Cir. 1986).

In Burdine the Supreme Court recognized the significance of credibility judgments by the trier of fact by noting that "there may be some cases where the plaintiff's initial evidence, combined with effective cross-examination of the defendant, will suffice to discredit the defendant's explanation" and that "this evidence and inferences properly drawn therefrom may be considered by the trier of fact on the issue of whether the defendant's explanation is pretextual." Id. at 255 n.10. Whether the proffered non-discriminatory reason is pretextual may turn on the jury's judgment as to the credibility of the witnesses "because almost every worker has some deficiency on which the employer can plausibly blame the worker's troubles." Hunter, supra, 797 F.2d at 1423.

The defendant argues that Mr. McKnight was fired because he did not meet the employer's legitimate job performance expectations. GM presented the testimony of numerous management personnel who held supervisory responsibilities over the plaintiff, along with the results of various personnel appraisals that evaluated the plaintiff in a negative manner. GM argues that the volume of this evidence was "overwhelming" and that Mr. McKnight did not provide a scintilla of evidence to prove that the allegations of employment performance deficiencies were pretextual. On the contrary, I find that the jury was presented with substantial evidence, which, if believed, would show that the defendant's proffered explanation of poor job performance was pretextual. First, the jury received the testimony of the plaintiff's expert on personnel practices. Dr. Dresang opined that the subjectivity of GM's employee appraisal system is such that it does not provide reliable evidence of poor performance. Second, the motives of a number of the defendant's witnesses who had supervisory responsibility for the plaintiff were effectively impeached. Some examples: one of the plaintiff's supervisors told racial jokes, using the word "nigger"; one of the plaintiff's supervisors was coerced into reducing an evaluation of Mr. McKnight's work performance; a former manufacturing superintendent provided an affidavit to the effect that the plaintiff's immediate supervisor wanted to terminate the plaintiff's employment for reasons unrelated to his job performance; and several black employees testified that they were concerned about how black employees were treated by Mr. McKnight's immediate supervisor. Third, assuming the validity of the defendant's negative appraisal of the plaintiff's job performance, there was evidence that the plaintiff was treated differently than others with similar performance problems.

Substantial evidence was offered by Mr. McKnight in support of his claim of retaliation. For example, Thomas Cassini admitted that the plaintiff's past litigation against the company was discussed in the meeting at which it was decided to fire the plaintiff; the plaintiff's immediate supervisor was told that he "must" document everything about the plaintiff because of the pending litigation; Mr. McKnight was referred to by a supervisor as a "hot potato" because of his litigation; there was evidence that supervisory personnel were upset with the plaintiff because he had filed complaints against the company; there was evidence that the plaintiff's assignment to "line 6" was retaliatory and designed to pave the way for his termination; and there was evidence that a supervisor repeatedly asked Mr. McKnight to sign a release for his complaint against the company and that this supervisor told him that his career at GM would be damaged if he did not sign.

The foregoing examples, along with other similar evidence offered at trial, are sufficient when viewed in the light most favorable to the plaintiff to have enabled the jury to reach the conclusion that the explanation offered by the defendant was pretextual. The findings of fact of the jury will not be disturbed.

The defendant's motion for a new trial is based on the following grounds: (a) that the jury's verdict is contrary to the great weight of the evidence; (b) that the defendant was denied a fair trial because of erroneous evidentiary rulings, the imposition of time constraints by the court, and alleged misconduct by the plaintiff's counsel; and (c) that the size of the damage award evinces bias and passion on the part of the jury which necessarily must have infected its determinations as to liability.

The authority to grant a new trial generally rests within the trial court's discretion. Allied Chemical Corp. v. Diaflon, Inc., 449 U.S. 33, 36 (1980). A new trial is warranted if the verdict is contrary to the clear weight of the evidence, if the damages award is excessive, or if the trial was not fair to the moving party. General Foam Fabricators, Inc. v. Tenneco Chemicals, Inc., 695 F.2d 281, 288 (7th Cir. 1982).

The defendant's allegations of misconduct by the plaintiff's attorney are singularly unfounded and merit no discussion.

The defendant lists fifteen evidentiary rulings by the court which it asserts were in error. The defendant wanted the court to limit the evidence to that which concerned the motives of only those management personnel directly involved in evaluating or supervising the plaintiff during the relevant time period. Such an evidentiary limitation is directly contrary to the approach reflected in McDonnell Douglas and would impose insurmountable evidentiary barriers on plaintiffs in this type of case. See Hunter, supra, 797 F.2d at 1423. I do not believe that the evidentiary rulings in this case prejudiced the defendant or justify a new trial.

The defendant argues that it was not given adequate time to present its case. At the pretrial conference both sides agreed that the trial would take no more than a week, and the court scheduled the case accordingly. Although this was not a complex case, it was tried with great zeal and competitiveness, and as the trial progressed it became very apparent that the presentation of proof was becoming unnecessarily prolonged. The allowable time provided to each side was then modified to accomplish the completion of the trial within the period originally contemplated; however, counsel were expressly informed that additional time would be afforded if the interests of justice required it. Indeed, at GM's request its allowable time was in fact extended near the end of the trial. GM never made an offer of proof as to what evidence it was unable to introduce and failed to make an objection as to the time allocations. Johnson v. Ashby, 808 F.2d 676, 678 (8th Cir. 1987). In my opinion, GM was afforded a full and adequate opportunity to present its case and my exercise of control over the length of the trial did not impinge on the defendants receiving a fair trial.

The jury's award of $55,000 for lost wages and fringe benefits was reasonable. The plaintiff earned wages of $32,000 for the eleven months that he worked for the defendant in 1983. After his discharge, Mr. McKnight earned $12,600 in 1984; $18,000 in 1985; $33,000 in 1986; $55,000 in 1987; and approximately $11,000 in 1988, up until the commencement of the trial. Accounting for lost benefits, projected salary increases and expenses incurred in commuting to Chicago in 1987, the $55,000 award was reasonable.

The jury's award of $55,000 for pain, suffering, and physical and emotional distress was also reasonable. A jury's assessment of damages for intangible harms such as humiliation and emotional distress is inherently subjective. I believe that the jury's judgment was amply supported by the evidence. The expert testimony of Dr. Lynch showed that the plaintiff suffered anxiety, sleep disorder, headaches and other psychosomatic complaints associated with stress, along with a loss of self-esteem as a result of his termination. The plaintiff was under such stress that just prior to his discharge, he sought psychiatric counseling. Dr. Lynch also testified that the plaintiff suffered a greater degree of emotional distress as a result of his termination than did the typical victim of unjust termination; this was because of the degree of investment that the plaintiff had made in terms of time and commitment to the defendant. Under these circumstances, an award of $55,000 is consistent with past awards for emotional distress in race discrimination cases under sec. 1981. eg. Foster v. MCI Telecommunications Corp., 555 F. Supp. 330 (D.C. Colo. 1983) ($50,000); Fisher v. Dillard University, 499 F.Supp. 525 (E.D. La. 1980) ($50,000); Williams v. Owens-Illinois, Inc., 25 F.E.P. Cases 1478 (N.D. Cal. 1979) ($50,000).

In my opinion, the jury's award of $500,000 for punitive damages is also reasonable. This is a case involving deliberate wrong doing by a wealthy defendant. There was ample evidence to enable the jury to conclude that GM intentionally retaliated against the plaintiff. An award of punitive damages is appropriate to punish a wrongdoer for its outrageous conduct and to deter others from engaging in similar conduct. Ramsely v. American Air Filter Co., 772 F.2d 1303, 1314 (7th Circ. 1985).

In order for an award to constitute meaningful punishment, the jury is permitted to take into account the size and wealth of the defendant. Simply because the amount necessary to constitute punishment and deterrence is sizable does not mean that the award of punitive damages is a windfall for the plaintiff. In that instant case, the award of punitive damages is not out of proportion to the amount of damages. It cannot be said that the amount of the award evidences that the jury was motivated by improper reasons, such as prejudice or caprice.

In his motion for reinstatement, Mr. McKnight argues that prevailing Title VII claimants are presumptively entitled to reinstatement. Donnellon v. Fruehauf, 794 F.2d 598 (11th Cir. 1986). The remedial purposes of the act contemplate that, in order to make the plaintiff whole, reinstatement may be granted. Albermarle Paper Co. v. Moody, 422 U.S. 405, 416 (1974). In that case the Supreme Court explained:

> It is true that backpay is not an automatic or mandatory remedy; like all other remedies under the Act, it is one which the courts "may" invoke. The scheme implicitly recognizes that there may be cases calling for one remedy but not another, and—owing to the structure of the federal judiciary—these choices are, of course, left in the first instance to the district courts.

Although the district court's discretion is equitable in nature, its judgment must be guided by the purposes of Title VII. Id. The purposes of Title VII are prophylactic:

[the purpose is] to achieve equality of employment opportunities and
to remove barriers that have operated in the past to favor an identifiable
group of white employees over other employees. [quoting Griggs v.
Duke Power Co., 401 U.S. 424, 429-30 (1971)] . . . It is also the purpose
of Title VII to make persons whole for injuries suffered on account of
unlawful employment discrimination. This is shown by the very fact
that Congress took care to arm the courts with full equitable powers.
For it is the historic purpose of equity to "secur[e] complete justice."
Albermarle, supra, at 417-18.

After balancing all the equities, I am convinced that reinstatement in this
case would not advance the purposes of Title VII. The plaintiff asserts that he
prefers not to be reinstated in his former position of manufacturing supervisor
but rather in a position concerned with corporate finance or investment banking.
Further, the evidence at trial established that the plaintiff has changed his career
goal from manufacturing management to being a stockbroker. I conclude that the
plaintiff does not have a primary interest in the position that he formerly held. At
trial it became evident that the relationship between the parties is acrimonious
at best and given the management level position involved, reinstatement would
probably be unproductive. It is clear that in the instant case the plaintiff has
been fully compensated and thereby made whole by the award of compensatory
damages, and the defendant has been properly punished by the award of punitive
damages. Complete justice requires no more in the context of the remedial
purpose of Title VII.

Therefore, IT IS ORDERED that the defendant's motions after verdict be
and hereby are denied.

IT IS ALSO ORDERED that the plaintiff's motion for reinstatement be
and hereby is denied.

Dated at Milwaukee, Wisconsin this _____ day of January, 1989.

Senior U.S. District Judge

Appendix E

Federal Employment Practice (FEP)
Federal Employment Practices Cases Volumes 52 thru 54, 1990-1991 and
Cummulative Digest.
Federal Employment Practice Cases Volumes 55 thru 57, 1991-1992 and
Cummulative Digest.

Appendix F

Title VII, 42 U.S. sec. 2000e-5

In Title VII, Congress has expressed an intention and provided that any person claiming to be aggrieved could bring suit under Title VII to challenge discriminatory employment practices. The legislative history indicates that Title VII was passed pursuant to the Commerce Clause of the Constitution. See U.S. Constitution Articles 1 & 8, Ch. 3. See 110 Congressional Record 7202-12, 8453-56, (1964); also, the legislative history cited in Heart of Atlanta Motel, Inc. v. United States, 379 U.S. 241, 245-46 (1964).

1   When we evaluate the relief awarded by the district court, we may look to both Title VII and DEA (Age Discrimination in Employment Act) cases. As we pointed out in Syvock v. Milwaukee Boiler Manufacturing Co., Inc., 665 F.2d 149, 162 n.19 (7th Cir. 1981), although Title VII and ADEA cases are "not necessarily automatically interchangeable in establishing the existence of discrimination, bith Title VII and ADEA vest trial courts with a similar broad discretion in awarding such legal or equitable relief as the courts deem appropriate." Id. (comparing 42 U.S.C. ss2000e-5(g) (1976) with 29 U.S.C. ss626(b) (1976).